Aunties

Book I received from my
Sweet neice Sara E Hall!
Wonderful Book for my 46th Birthday.

pg 21 Blueberry Pie
pg 31 Priest Story
pg. 47 Lesbian Aunt
108. Ravioli (easy)

Aunties

THIRTY-FIVE WRITERS CELEBRATE
THEIR OTHER MOTHER

Edited by Ingrid Sturgis

BALLANTINE BOOKS NEW YORK

A Ballantine Book
Published by The Random House Publishing Group

Copyright © 2004 by Ingrid Sturgis

Owing to limitations of space, permission acknowledgments can be found
on pages 205–206, which constitute an extension of this copyright page.

www.ballantinebooks.com

Library of Congress Cataloging-in-Publication Data

Aunties : thirty-five writers celebrate their other mother / edited by Ingrid Sturgis.—1st ed.
p.   cm.
ISBN 0-345-45269-0
1. Authors, American—20th century—Family relationships. 2. Authors, American—21st
century—Family relationships. 3. Aunts—United States—Biography. I. Sturgis, Ingrid.
PS135.A94 2004
810.9'005—dc22
[B]   2003065560

Manufactured in the United States of America

First Edition: May 2004

10 9 8 7 6 5 4 3 2 1

Book design by Carole Lowenstein

Contents

Handwritten note: 3/2006 Sarn gave me for my 46th B-Day [signature] Major

New York Aunties

Role Models

Avenging Angels

Acknowledgments

I thank all the writers who contributed to *Aunties* for their generous spirit and wonderful stories. It could not have been completed without their support and enthusiasm. I'd like to thank my editors Elisabeth Dyssegaard, who guided me along, and Julia Cheiffetz, who nudged me along. Thanks also to my agent, Denise Stinson, and to Anita Diggs, who delivered this project as a gift. Thanks also to my mother, Ozia, a great aunt in her own right, and my husband, Ed, a great uncle (That's another book!), and my sisters, who could inspire auntie stories all their own.

Introduction

Aunties celebrates those unsung heroines who step into our lives bringing joy, unconditional love, support, and sometimes confusion. An aunt can be like your other mother or a protective older sister. Or she can be much more.

When I told friends that I was writing about aunties, many spontaneously told me stories of the women who touched their lives in meaningful ways. One said her aunt Bert is everybody's aunt, a title earned because of the matriarchal role she assumed as a teen. At an age when most girls are dating, Aunt Bert was already the rock of her family. She dropped out of school at sixteen to raise her siblings when her mother died in childbirth. Even after she married, Aunt Bert stayed home to run the household while her father worked two jobs to support the family. She raised her three children while raising her siblings.

Another friend's aunt Georgeanna was tough as nails, and held on to her money with a tight fist. Georgeanna outlived all but one sister, and swore to her niece that she would never die. But Georgeanna eventually succumbed in her nineties, leaving her niece with what she loved the most—her money.

For Wally "Famous" Amos, his aunt Della's baking was his key to success. Amos told me that he could just about taste her chocolate chip cookies when he reminisces about licking the bowl and spoon in his aunt's cozy kitchen, also a place of refuge after his parents' divorce. He never imagined that this simple pleasure would become a national culinary hit. Amos eventually lost his original cookie company through bad managerial decisions, but he has returned once again to the source of his inspiration, naming a new cookie company for Aunt Della.

I've been blessed with five aunts, but it is with my aunt Mildred that I have a special connection. Both Virgos, we are kindred spirits who share a creative bent and unconventional style. Mildred encouraged my endeavors when I studied art in college. In fact, she is the one who encouraged me to follow my heart and leave teaching to become a journalist. Trained as a nurse, Mildred always seemed ready for adventure, whether it was moving with her husband and family from one part of the country to another, or creating and selling rag dolls or opening a store. I still remember how she came to New York for my wedding and spent that night whipping up a big pot of peas and rice for the next day's reception buffet. But what I love most about my aunt is that she mirrored my affection and helped to validate my aspirations when I wasn't sure I was entitled to them.

Thirty-five writers have contributed stories and poetry to *Aunties* that bridge the cultural spectrum and offer common themes about the women who may have forged a path, inspired careers, filled in for a mother or even a father. These aunties enthusiastically served as cheerleaders, mentors, or friends, helping their nieces and nephews navigate the often-troubled shoals of family life.

The collection is organized into five sections: Second Mothers, Independent Spirits, New York Aunties, Role Models, and Avenging Angels. The Second Mothers are the shaking and baking, nurturing aunts who picked up where a mom or dad might have left off. They unflinchingly take on the parental role for children already buffeted by life's challenges. Independent Spirits includes aunts who live life off the grid, cutting a wide swath, often across cultures, compelling their nieces or nephews to follow. They may not always be right, but they are never dull, and their lives hold instruction for those who find convention too confining.

New York Aunties features the surprising number of stories about thoroughly modern aunts who exemplify the swagger, attitude, and survival instinct of that city. These often larger-than-life characters singlehandedly traverse the subways, careers, and family responsibilities. Role Models are the women whose exemplary life offers rules to live by. They mix strength, resilience, and fortitude with a dollop of love. Avenging Angels are the fearless women who erect a defensive armor to protect their nieces and nephews from harm and often family hurts.

Unfortunately, there is little research about the family role these unsung heroines play. And despite an aunt's place within families, she really exists outside the nuclear family, where she can offer relationships free of parental constraints and a safe place to learn about the larger village. With little regard for the rewards of motherhood, an aunt accepts her often-tenuous role with nieces and nephews, enriching them all the same.

As Candace Hardnett wrote me about her aunt Carolyn: "Too often, the auntie goes unmentioned; the importance of her role in the family is not always recognized. We celebrate Mother's Day and Father's Day, but where is Auntie's Day?"

I offer this book as a loving tribute to make your auntie's day.

Second Mothers

Laundry

SANDE BORITZ BERGER

My great aunt Irene is the oldest living relative in our family, the only link to a past that began in a tiny shtetl in Lithuania over a century ago. A petite Clairol blonde nearing ninety, Irene is visiting my home on Long Island for the weekend. It's a little past nine on this Friday night, when she taps on my bedroom door, simultaneously apologizing for the intrusion.

"Come in, come in," I say, hoping to convince her she's welcome. She approaches my bed balancing a leaning tower of clean laundry she has finished folding. Somehow, laundry touched by my aunt's warm hands never needs pressing. There is something magical in the way she arranges all things domestic, never a loose thread or speck of dust to be found in the tidy world she inhabits.

"Tired, Mommele?" she asks, using an endearment I remember from childhood. I see her gazing around my disheveled room as if searching for survivors of a twister. A week's worth of clothing is strewn over the backs of chairs, and books stacked like dominoes sit on the night table. But I don't feel judged by her: not now, not ever. I relax back on my corduroy reading pillow and motion for her to come sit near me on the edge of the bed.

"Why is he so late?" my aunt asks, still standing, squinting at the digital clock radio. I tell her that my husband had a dinner meeting and she shouldn't worry so much. I stifle a laugh when instantly reminded of the roots of my own paranoia. There is doom and disaster stamped into her light brown pupils.

"Do you want I should put away the clothing?"

"No thank you, just plop it all on top of the dresser. And please, sit down."

She walks slowly, kneeling with the pile as if she were bearing gifts to royalty. I wonder what makes her so comfortable with servitude as she carefully creates a temporary home for the laundry at the edge of my dresser.

Again, her eyes peruse the room. I think she is stalling and really wants to talk. I shimmy my body over to make more room for her. She slips off a beautiful pair of beige leather pumps, and examines them. As a child, I was constantly trying on her shoes and begging her to save them for me. She promised, but one summer my feet grew two sizes larger than hers.

"Will you save those for my Jenny?" I ask, grinning. But she's distracted and doesn't seem to connect to my wave of nostalgia. "Auntie, do you need a pair of slippers?"

"No, darling, I'm fine." She's come prepared for this visit with her chintz housecoat, a relic from the 1950s, terry-cloth slippers, pink plastic hair rollers, and several washcloths. She knows my two teenage girls and I walk around in our underwear, and use cotton balls to clean our faces and noisy hair blowers to dry our hair.

It's only a few hours since her arrival, and already she's emptied the refrigerator of fuzzy unrecognizable objects, polished the flatware, and refolded every towel in the linen closet. Her pink mottled hands look years older than her face, and her fingers are gnarled from years of fixing and touching. My aunt has the soul of an immigrant, always anxious to earn her keep. I imagine this stems from the many years she spent living under the roof of her brother (my grandfather), after he sent the money for her and her older and only sister to come to America. When she was still just a teenager, in his home, she baked, cleaned, and cooked, helping to prepare elaborate Sabbath dinners, which were a family ritual every Friday evening.

"I miss him," she says, unexpectedly bursting into tears.

"Who?" I ask, dazed, thinking of my husband, still at the office, and why his being late would make her cry.

"My Fred," she whimpers, pulling a tissue from her sleeve before I grab one from the box. It's nearly ten years since her husband passed away. They'd married just months after being fixed up by a family friend. Uncle Fred was in the army; he had the job of recruiting men and women for the Reserves because he spoke several languages. Already well into their forties, they decided not to have children. Instead they filled their lives with work and doted on their three nieces and six nephews, whom they visited often. Every August, they traveled abroad to see Uncle Fred's relatives, who lived in Wiesbaden, Germany. It was their only real luxury, since Uncle Fred made a modest living working in the royalties department of a publishing company.

When I was young, I imagined them as the couple you'd see on top of a wedding cake, nearly perfect. They lived snug and content in a studio apartment for more than thirty years. Even now, my aunt sleeps on the same Castro convertible they opened every night before going to bed.

"Oh, Auntie, I know you do," I say, taking her trembling hand in mine. Has she waited weeks or months to cry with someone she feels close to? My aunt has always been too proud to share her grief with neighbors or casual friends.

There was a time during my highly emotional, misunderstood teenage years when she was there for me while I cried. Whenever possible, my aunt shielded me from my mother's quick temper or my father's tough-love discipline. Either by telephone or in person, when hearing of my minor misdeeds, she would quietly interfere, spouting off my good virtues as if she was reading the ingredients of a favorite recipe. Sometimes just her words were enough to get me a reduced sentence in my punishments, which were usually because I talked back—which I always thought talking was all about.

My mother, a social butterfly of the postwar era, often left me in Aunt Irene's meticulous care. I was a toddler when we walked hand in hand on busy Brooklyn streets, stopping at fish markets and butcher shops with the distinctive aroma of sawdust floors. We'd sit for hours on splintery wooden benches in tree-lined parks, my aunt introducing me to people who only smiled. She bought me special gifts with the money she earned working in my grandfather's knitting plant, showing each new season's line to the out-of-town buyers, and taking orders: white cotton gloves, felt hats, and expensive velvet-collared dresses, perfect for taking me to a matinee performance of the Rockettes at Radio City Music Hall. With her compassionate words, she has painted pictures of a childhood happier than I remember. Even now, over forty, I hunger for the retelling of those stories, the insatiable need to glimpse again at that joyful child.

She stops crying as quickly as she began, then reaches out for an oversized neon-colored sweatshirt I'd thrown over the bedpost. "Can you get me one like this?" she asks. It's so electrically bright, I can't believe she likes it.

"Sure," I say, straight-faced. "I'll ask my girlfriend who makes them."

"Maybe in a softer shade of green," she says, taking another deep sigh. A few seconds later she says, "Ach, I should probably move to Florida."

My mother has been badgering her, for years, to move down south. But I know my aunt. Unlike the Dodgers she once worshiped, she will never, ever leave Brooklyn, or the antiques-laden apartment she has rented all these years.

"I don't know how your mother can stand those ceramic classes with all those yentas . . . sitting there, day after day, making those ridiculous ashtrays and clowns, breathing in all that powdery dust," she says, shielding her nose and mouth.

I can't help but laugh. She's got a point. I, myself, am overstocked with faux Lladros and misshapen serving bowls. But my mother is protected by the banality of ceramic making. It gives her something to look forward to. She still has my father, a sometimes-amicable companion. Though she may be lonely, unlike my aunt, she's not alone.

"I can talk to you," I say. "I never talked to Mom this easily."

"Your mother means well, honey," she answers, now defending her elder niece.

"It's just that she has nothing really important to discuss." She turns both her palms up like a magician. "Nothing."

"She can still drive me crazy." I'm sulking like a five-year-old, wishing that this little old woman on the edge of my bed were my mother.

"Are you sure you're not my real mother?"

She giggles. Then gets sullen, her mouth quivering. "You were like my child; I took you everywhere. People would stop me in elevators, talk to you, and say, What a personality! Uncle Fred, he knew, he said you'd be someone special."

Tears fall on my cheeks. And I wonder if there will ever be a time when I no longer hunger for this kind of validation, whether my aunt was the true giver of unconditional love.

"Oh, I didn't mean to upset you," she says.

"It's okay, really. I'm fine."

The front door slams. We hear my husband's loud footsteps downstairs in the kitchen. My aunt picks up her shoes and scurries toward the bedroom door.

"Good night," I say, blowing my nose, afraid that saying "I love you" would cause me to choke on the hard lump forming at the back of my throat.

I wish I could give her something, anything, as she reaches the threshold of my bedroom door. "Take this, Auntie, please," I say, jumping from the bed and draping the neon sweatshirt over her arm. It occurs to me that she has never asked me for anything—that she takes pride in her independence now more than ever. To my surprise, she takes the shirt and clutches it to her chest. Falling back on my pillow, I memorize my aunt's fading silhouette. She leaves behind a faint aroma of lilacs, much like the clean sweetness of freshly folded laundry.

Sande Boritz Berger

My Other Mother

SARAH BRACEY WHITE

In grade school, most of the kids I knew wrote letters to Santa or prayed to God when they wanted something. I wrote to Aunt Susie, my mother's sister in Philadelphia. Aunt Susie's influence on me has been as powerful as that of my mother. Family lore has it that she was even responsible for my name. Before my birth, she told my mother, "You've already got three daughters, and you haven't named any of them after our dead mother. If this one's a girl, you've got to name her Sarah." And Mama did.

My first memories are of Aunt Susie's basement; I lived with her then. I was almost five years old and standing at one end of a long wooden table, dressing and undressing paper dolls. She was at the other end, stacking freshly ironed sheets, wrapping the bundles with brown paper secured by tape that she moistened on a shiny metal dispenser. Every now and then, passing neighbors would say hello through two small windows set at street level, just above the flatwork ironer Aunt Susie operated with a foot pedal. I was comforted by the contraption's familiar hiss, a sound that I remembered hearing from the time I was nine months old.

As a child, I loved Aunt Susie more than anyone else in the whole world, and she treated me like the sun. Each morning when I would run into her room, she would ask, "What did you dream last night?" as she mulled over her "dream book," trying to divine the winning number combination that would make her a rich woman.

Aunt Susie hit the number a lot; when she did, she'd buy me something special on our next shopping trip. On Thursdays, her day off from her laundry business, we'd put on our Sunday clothes and ride the green-and-yellow trolley downtown. After lunch, which featured our favorite dish of macaroni and cheese at the Horn & Hardart Automat, we'd walk around and look at all the pretty things in the store windows. Sometimes we'd go to the Chapeau on Walnut Street, where the owner always welcomed us with smiles. "She's so friendly," my aunt would whisper, "because she knows I'm a sucker for her expensive hats."

Next, we'd go to John Wanamaker's, Aunt Susie's favorite department store. We usually made a beeline for the children's department, where I would show Aunt Susie the dresses I liked. She would finger them without buying anything, saying, "They're overpriced." But I was never unhappy because I knew that Mrs. Smith, the dressmaker who lived upstairs over Nix Funeral Home on the corner of our block, would soon be fitting me with an outfit just like them.

Once Aunt Susie spotted a white fur jacket with a matching pillbox hat and muff on display in the window of a children's store. When we went inside and asked to see the outfit, the white saleslady told her it was too expensive. Aunt Susie glared at the woman and told her that she could buy anything she damn well wanted. The saleslady turned beet red as Aunt Susie counted out the money for all three pieces. I showed Uncle Will my new ensemble when we got home and told him what happened. He laughed and said, "Susie's mouth is gonna get her in trouble yet." Aunt Susie just laughed. "The reason I moved up north was so my mouth wouldn't get me in trouble. And I don't intend to let anybody, colored or white, disrespect me."

She seemed to know everything, although she only went through the eighth grade. After school, Aunt Susie worked alongside her mama, washing clothes for white families. By the time she was twenty-two, she had moved to Philadelphia, picking the City of Brotherly Love, she said, because she needed some loving after all those years of bad treatment down south.

At first my aunt worked in a laundry downtown, but after she married Uncle Will, they bought a four-bedroom row house in North Philadelphia, and she started a laundry business in the basement. Aunt Susie took in only flat goods—sheets, pillowcases, table linen, and curtains—because she never wanted to touch the smelly old clothes of strangers ever again. She told me that I would never have to do this kind of work because I was going to college.

All of her sisters and brothers stayed with her at one time or another. Everybody except my mama, who never liked living up north because she said there were too many people, too much noise, and too many beer gardens. Still, every summer Mama would come up from South Carolina to visit us. And Aunt Susie would tell me to be extra nice to Mama because she loved me a lot, too.

She always called herself a city girl who loved hoagies, especially Philly cheesesteaks, with lots of fried onions, and hot cherry peppers on the side. Sometimes she'd send a neighborhood boy to buy one at Hoagie Heaven around the corner on Sixteenth Street.

I never liked them.

"All the more for me," she would say, licking her lips and fingers, then washing everything down with a root beer.

Aunt Susie was old enough to be my grandmother because she was sixteen when my mama was born. Mama and Aunt Susie hardly looked alike, except when they smiled, but Mama never smiled. She was a head shorter than Aunt Susie, light-skinned, like the color of the milk with watered-down coffee that Aunt Susie would let me drink. Mama had natural thick black curls unlike Aunt Susie's, whose curls came from a curling iron. Whenever I spied a gray hair in Aunt Susie's head, she'd cuss and then pull it out. Mama never cussed or even talked loud. She said it was unladylike. She also said Aunt Susie shouldn't be playing the numbers because it was illegal. But Aunt Susie just laughed and said, "White folks make the law and they play the numbers, so why shouldn't I?"

Mama pinched her lips tight whenever my aunt talked about white folks. Aunt Susie would say it's because Mama lived down south and didn't understand that white folks weren't any better than black folks.

Sometimes while ironing, Aunt Susie would tell me how I came to live with her. She said after my daddy ran off and left us, Mama needed to go back to work as a third-grade teacher. My three older sisters were school age, but I was only six months old, and there was nobody to care for me.

"Me and Will always dreamed of having children, but I couldn't have children, while your mama spit out babies like watermelon seeds," Aunt Susie would say. "Me and Will adopted a little girl and named her

Loretta. Before Loretta's fourth birthday, she got a real bad fever. My alcohol baths couldn't break it. We took her to the hospital, and the doctor said her appendix had burst. In a few days, she died. I was so lonely. I begged your mama to let you come live with me until you got old enough to start school. She said okay, and I took the train to South Carolina to get you." Aunt Susie would stop what she was doing to hug me real tight, then say, "And you've been my little girl ever since."

When the sun went down, Aunt Susie would sit out front on the steps while I played with the other kids. She never talked much to the neighbors because she said when people know all your business they start getting in it, and she never wanted anybody in her business. She always told me not to repeat the stuff that went on in our house. Once when I told my friend Frankie Henderson that she was rich, Aunt Susie wouldn't let me go out to play for a whole week. She said it was a lesson to teach me to curb my tongue.

The summer I was five and a half, I overheard Mama and Aunt Susie talking in loud voices during one of Mama's visits. "Sarah's getting out of hand, Sister. You're not teaching her proper respect for grown people—she talks to them like she's their equal."

"Aw, don't be so old-fashioned," Aunt Susie reasoned. "She just ain't scared of grown folks like we were."

"But that's not all. When I said her dress was pretty, she said, 'Thank you, I know it!' You and Will spoil her rotten."

"Oh, you're gettin' all upset over nothing."

"I don't want to argue with you, Sister. We never see eye to eye. I appreciate everything you've done to help me, but Philadelphia's not for me—or my children. I want to take Sarah home."

What was my mother talking about? This was my home! I inched my way down the staircase. It creaked, and their voices fell silent. I ran back to my room, certain that Aunt Susie would never let me go.

When Mama left Philadelphia without me a few days later, I felt relieved until I asked Aunt Susie whether my sister Williette stayed behind because she was going to live with us, too.

Her eyes filled with tears. "No. Your sister is going to take you home at the end of the month."

"But don't you love me anymore?" I asked.

"You're not going home because I don't love you, Sarah. You're going home because your mama loves you, too."

"But I want to live here! Make her let me stay here."

"I can't do that. She brought you in this world, and she decides where you live."

When I began to cry, Aunt Susie took me on her lap and tried to console me. Nothing eased my sorrow. It was as if I was being cast out of the Garden of Eden.

"Will you get a new little girl to keep you company after I'm gone?" I asked Aunt Susie as she tucked me in the night before my departure.

"No, honey, I don't think God intends for me to have a little girl of my own," she said.

"Will you forget about me?"

"How could I forget you?" Aunt Susie asked. "Think of all the things we've done together and the places we been—and all those pictures I've got of you. I'll be thinking about you all the time. When you learn to write, you can send me letters and tell me what you're doing. I bet you'll just love it down there."

"No, I won't! I'm a city girl," I cried.

The next day, Uncle Will and Aunt Susie took Williette and me to the North Philadelphia depot. When the train pulled in, the four of us climbed on board. Aunt Susie put three new books of paper dolls next to me, on top of the shoebox with our lunch in it. "Now you be good and listen to your sister," she said. "She's in charge until you get home." Then, she bent low for a last hug.

"I don't want to go," I whispered.

"And I don't want you to go," she answered. "But sometimes we got to do things we don't want to do. This is one of those times, so be brave and remember, I'll be thinking of you."

"All aboard," the conductor announced.

"We got to go now," Aunt Susie said. "You stay in your seat, Sarah, and be a good girl."

Aunt Susie and Uncle Will left the train. Outside, she turned and waved once, then walked away.

Memories of the life I shared with Aunt Susie sustained me long after I returned to South Carolina, where I chafed under my family's poverty and the Jim Crow way of life. But no matter how degrading white people in Sumter treated my mother, my sisters, or me, I knew that they were wrong in their judgment of us. My aunt Susie had made me certain of my own value, long before James Brown sang "I'm Black and I'm Proud." One day, I knew that I, too, would escape the South and live a life like hers.

From a distance, Aunt Susie was my family's guardian angel. When one of us was sick, she wired money for the doctor and medicine. Sometimes the money orders she tucked in her letters paid the light bill or the rent. If my sisters or I needed something extra for school or after-school programs, all we had to do was write to Aunt Susie.

Most summers, my mother still sent my sisters and me to Philadelphia to visit Aunt Susie. Though I was always glad to see her, I stayed aloof from the love she tried to give me. I felt that she had replaced me with the foster children she took in after I left, as I had replaced Loretta. I never thought about how hard it must have been for her to lose me.

She hid her sadness well but never stopped loving me or supporting all my dreams. My mother's death a few months before my high school graduation filled Aunt Susie with a sadness I had never seen before. At Mama's funeral, she kept repeating, "I was supposed to go first." Days after my graduation, I received a letter from her containing a sheet of blue-lined notebook paper, a train ticket, a twenty-dollar bill, and a shiny brochure.

Dear Sarah,

I got you a summer job! My friend Claudia Lee from around the corner is the cook at a fancy white girls' camp up in Vermont. She says you can be her helper. The job pays $300 plus train fare, room, and board. Wish I could of had a chance like this when I was your age. I had to pick cotton or take care of white folks' babies. This is a real opportunity. I'm sending you a little spending money for the trip here. See you soon.

Love, Aunt Susie

Once again, Aunt Susie had come to my rescue. I didn't know much about cooking, but before that summer was over, her friend had turned me into a respectable one. That summer I also learned a lot about people and life. Those lessons still serve me today. When I graduated

Sarah Bracey White

from college, Aunt Susie was there. "See, you made it! Just like I said you would," she said, grinning proudly.

Years later, when I self-published a book of poetry, Aunt Susie requested two dozen copies. She sold them to all her neighbors and friends, then mailed me a check for $150. "I'm so proud of you. Can't wait until your next book comes out. One day you'll be famous."

During a phone call, I told her that I could never be famous because famous people have lots of baby pictures and I had none. The next time I visited, she handed me a box. "Now, you have no reason not to be famous." Inside, was a cache of photos taken during my years living with her. Shortly before Aunt Susie's death, I went to Philadelphia to visit her. After preparing dinner, I insisted that we eat in the dining room, using her good china, silver, and linens. "Where did you get to be so fancy, young lady?" she teased.

"I learned it from you, Aunt Susie," I answered. "You've made me who I am."

In Search of Silver

TARA L. MASIH

Almora, India, 1989—It's my last full day in Almora, and I'm on a quest. My companion is Lilly Auntie, her stocky shape draped with a colorful sari that ripples with purpose as she moves forward into the bazaar. In search of the jewelers' alley, we pass by plastic Day-Glo *chappals*, compact umbrellas, electronic equipment, all amid colorful bangles and hammered copperware. The silversmith alley used to be crowded with stalls and teeming with bargainers. But the Almora smiths, known for the silver they spin into intricate, filigreed designs, are fast disappearing, as are many of the small-crafts people in India. They are giving up their burlap-covered stalls for the mass-producing factories in the cities that export all craftwork, including jewelry, in bulk quantities to foreign countries.

I don't know whether I'll return to my father's hometown in the Himalayan foothills. And if I do, I worry about what I'll find—an ancient bazaar-turned-flea-market, where Ty animals; T-shirts covered with innocuous, even offensive slogans; cell phones; and discount toiletries are all peddled by merchants working only for profit.

I speak no Hindi, and although Lilly Auntie understands English, she is shy about speaking it. Our conversations have consisted of my talking and her nodding sweetly, her gold earrings tinkling. But yesterday at the house, when she heard I wanted to find a silversmith, she smiled like I had just paid her a compliment. She turned to another relative, who translated: "Lilly will take you to bazaar tomorrow." I was relieved to have a guide who spoke the language.

My father's ancestors represented a clan from the Kshatriya (ruler and warrior) caste that originated in the central desert region of Rajputana, known as the land of the Rajputs. When Moslems invaded from the North, they drove the Rajput clans to the safe, rolling bosoms of the Himalayan foothills, a natural fortress. Even today the paved roads that hug the mountainsides in hairpin formations are treacherous and wash out in monsoon season, making them impassable. And in these hills, really mountains, just miles south of Nepal and Tibet, you can see that mixing has occurred in the slight slant of Asian features in some of my family members.

I see it in the photos of my grandmother, Dadi. There are pictures of her holding me in her garden in the bright Indian sun. A two-year-old in a handmade slip of a dress, I never saw her again. I have stories from my parents about her generous spirit (the entire town attended her funeral), her strength in standing up to my brilliant, strong-willed Dada. I know I'm her height—small at five-foot-one.

And I see Dadi's face in Lilly Auntie's, see the same hair color and hairline, dark strands pulled to the center of the back of the head in a round bun. The resemblance is so strong I assume they were sisters, forgetting that in India everyone is Auntie or Uncle, so I never question calling her Lilly Auntie and assume she is my great-aunt. I hold her in the place of my dadi, feel as if I am with a grandmother in the van that ferries us to the bazaar the next day.

Once there the driver deposits us at the base of the hill where the road begins to the outdoor market. Lilly takes to the cobblestoned street like a freshly coiled spring, youthful energy in each step up and into the center.

After several stops for directions, we find the alley that now holds only two jewelers. Lilly quickly assesses and chooses, points me toward a turbaned man sitting cross-legged on the ground. I know what I want, and the jeweler isn't pleased. He knows I am unmarried, and he doesn't want to sell me the *mangala sutra*—the necklace worn by Indian women once they are married, often the focal point of Hindu marriage ceremonies. I'll be wearing it in the States, so what will it matter?

It matters to him, descendant in a long line of patriarchal predecessors. But my quiet aunt shows the determination of Dadi and speaks firmly. Round one is won, and the jeweler reluctantly pulls out a necklace of black beads doubled and roped together by alternating, almost-pure silver rosettes. He is to inset the rosettes and wants me to choose the usual red or green glass. I hate primary colors. I try to express, through Lilly, that I want clear glass to mimic diamonds. Round two—somehow the lack of bright color offends his creative, Eastern sensibilities. My aunt speaks more forcefully, and their Hindi rises and falls like furious music in male and female disharmony, until finally he relents. With my finished necklace in a paper-covered box, we leave—giggling in complicity—a very grumpy artisan.

Indians are passionate and allowed to show emotion, even expected to emote sorrow. Thus, good-byes are hard and exhausting to make in India. When a family member leaves the country, everyone hovers, shivaree-like, around the one returning overseas. Close relatives, distant relatives, servants, sometimes even townspeople one doesn't know or met only in passing make their farewells. Trips to India are expensive and physically demanding and therefore infrequent. Visits occur in a contracted sense of time. Hanging above everyone is the fear that they'll never see one another again.

It's hard to say good-bye to Lilly Auntie. Her shyness toward me is mostly gone now, too late for us to have any extended conversations. I enfold her generous girth, feel her softness through the thin sweater covering her sari, smell the sandalwood soap on her skin. She steps back and hands me a small plastic box with a clear lid that reveals a silver, paisley-shaped pendant, an archaic symbol that originated in India. There is a twinkle in her eye. She must have purchased it when I wasn't looking.

But this story is not about jewelry. It's about a woman who happily slipped into the place of the grandmother who couldn't be there, who made sure her aunt's granddaughter left India with something important, a piece of heritage. And she gave me a glimpse of the strong spirit my grandmother must have been. I am not sure if such gifts of spirit are carried on the intricate strands of genes or adopted through the more subtle exchange of shared experience, but they do, most certainly, carry on.

Tara L. Masih

Blueberry Memories

WILLIAM C. DAVIS

"Do you smell it yet, June?" Aunt Belle asked. "Yes," I replied. "Another few minutes and it'll be done," she smiled.

I still remember the aroma of blueberries simmering in sugar and spices. My sister Francine and I could barely contain ourselves as we waited for Aunt Belle's signature blueberry pie. What made the pie special were the fresh blueberries we picked that grew wild on bushes in wooded areas behind the homes on Hatch Street. Aunt Belle showed me how to pick the berries when they were ripe and warned me to watch out for the black widow spiders that lurked in the bushes. I was always very careful not to get bitten. I picked the berries and put them in little square boxes and rushed home. I loved to watch her wash the berries, dry them, and mix the ingredients for the pie.

Memories like this were typical of my early childhood spent in the Devencrest area of Ayer, Massachusetts—as were the harsh New England winters, spent sleeping under a quilt and hearing the lonesome train whistle in the distance. Aunt Belle was an army wife. Her husband, Uncle Wash, was an army master sergeant stationed at Fort Devens, Massachusetts.

Aunt Belle was the middle of four sisters—Aunt Fannie Bea Mabry was the oldest; next came Aunt Selma. My mother, Barbara, was the youngest girl. There were also four brothers—the oldest was Felton, then Curtis, Carlton, whom I resemble, and Lorenzo. The head of the Mabry clan were Robert and Rosa, my grandparents. My mother, Barbara Mabry Davis, and my aunt Belle Mabry Washington were close all their lives.

Aunt Belle's place was a sanctuary for Francine and me in the early 1940s after my father died when I was two years old. My mother lived in Harlem and found it difficult raising two children without any help. As a young boy, I spent more time in Ayer while my sister Francine stayed home with Mother. To this day I don't know why Aunt Belle called me June; maybe it was short for Junior. Because of my age, I could travel to Ayer on the New York Central railroad for free. Most of the time I rode with my cousin Curtis, who was six years older. We usually went in late spring or winter.

I had lots of friends to play with in Ayer because most of the people on Hatch Street were army families. Aunt Belle and Uncle Wash would tell me about the places they had lived. She was a nurse and often told stories about working in hospitals in different states.

My aunt was an accomplished cook who really enjoyed fixing food for us—turkey, chicken, collard greens, black-eyed peas, crackling bread, and my favorite, blueberry pie. After dinner I watched as she crocheted doilies or knitted a blanket. She once knitted for me a green vest with buttons that I cherished and wore for years. It never wore out; I eventually got too big for it. Aunt Belle was like a second mother to us. She had a quiet and pleasant way and was always even tempered; I never saw her angry. When she would ask me to run an errand for her, I did so willingly because she asked me so nicely. She seemed to be at peace with herself and made me feel her life was made more complete when I came around.

About 1947, Uncle Wash retired from the army and they moved to Beck Street in the Bronx. They bought a three-story brick home with a nice patch of green in the rear that they made into a flower garden. They lived on the ground level and rented out the two upper floors.

I remember helping them move in when I was only eleven. I was so excited because they were now close by, and I could take the subway to my second home in the Bronx. I spent many nights there, especially from 1950 to 1954, when I was in high school. My family lived on the third floor of a six-story tenement apartment house that had no elevator on West 138th Street in Harlem. Fires were common in the hallway dumbwaiter, which was used to transport trash to the basement, and we had to evacuate our apartment several times over the years. When the firemen came, the first thing they would do was to turn off the electricity. Sometimes it was off for two or three days. When this happened,

William C. Davis

I would gather my schoolbooks, dash to the subway, and drop a dime in the turnstile. I'd arrive at Aunt Belle's within an hour.

On weekends, Aunt Belle would take me shopping on 149th Street. We shopped at Hearn's meat market, where Aunt Belle pointed out the best place to get fresh high-quality meats, especially pork chops. In the evenings, we'd watch television—Milton Berle, Ed Sullivan, Sid Caesar, and Imogene Coca. But nothing was more rewarding than listening to Aunt Belle talk about her parents. She told me how Rosa would look after her sons Emerson and Curtis when she went to work. She told me about her brothers and sisters, and life growing up in Russell County, Alabama. I would listen for hours as she told stories in her soft voice about the games they played. It was through Aunt Belle's storytelling that I learned about our family roots. I found a sense of pride and strength knowing about my ancestors, which spurred me on to make something of myself. Aunt Belle encouraged me to follow my heart and not just to stay in school but also to set goals and excel in my studies.

She inspired me to go to college like my cousins Emerson and Curtis did. I went on to obtain an associate degree in electrical technology, a bachelor's in English, and a master's degree in communication arts.

Although Uncle Wash spent close to thirty years in the army and retired as a master sergeant, Aunt Belle told me the only job that he was able to get as a civilian was as a messenger for a Wall Street firm. But she said he never griped or complained. He smiled as he delivered important messages to firms in lower Manhattan. I never could understand why Uncle Wash couldn't get something more in line with his army experience.

Aunt Belle told me that times would change and get better for me. She always told me to hold my head high and not to become embittered about racism. I heeded her advice, and when racism came my way, I confronted it and moved on, without drowning in self-pity.

As the years went by I would visit her in the Bronx occasionally, and she would have a signature pie ready with frozen blueberries. Mother died in 1969 and Belle in 1991. When I reminisce about Aunt Belle, I remember most of all her warmth and encouragement. I was twice blessed, with two mothers. Her love and nurturing gave me so much confidence that I felt I could do anything I set my mind to. I miss the comfort of her presence. Her guiding spirit has always made my life feel complete.

Aunt Belle's Easy Blueberry Pie

3 tablespoons flour
¾ cup sugar
¼ teaspoon ground cinnamon
4 cups fresh blueberries, washed and patted dry with paper towels
½ teaspoon lemon juice

PIE CRUST
2 frozen 9-inch deep-dish pie shells
1 to 2 tablespoons butter or margarine

Combine flour, sugar, and cinnamon in a large bowl. Stir mixture with a rubber spatula. Add blueberries and lemon juice. Gently fold blueberries well into mixture. Thaw uncovered pie shells for 15 minutes at room temperature. Pour combined mixture into one shell. Dot mixture on four sides with 1 to 2 tablespoons of butter or margarine.

Loosen second pie shell from tin and place crust over pie mixture. Now gently loosen and remove pie tin from crust. Press curved part of a fork all around pie crust to close any spaces between the two crusts. Last, poke a hole in middle of crust and at five or six other places.

Bake in preheated oven at 400 degrees F for 30 minutes, then decrease to 350 degrees for 20 minutes. Pie is done when crust is a golden brown. Remove and let cool for 30 minutes.

William C. Davis

Aunt Bessie's Secret Life

REBECCA McCLANAHAN

The night Aunt Bessie arrived, I was sitting cross-legged on my bed, re-viewing the events leading up to World War II for a test the next day. When I heard gravel in the driveway, I walked to the window and lifted a slat on the venetian blinds. Dad was opening the door to the passen-ger side, and from the light of the porch, I saw her emerge. In a few minutes she stood in the doorway of my room, holding a brown suit-case, layered like an exiled Jew from the pages of my history book, her navy blue wool coat stuffed so tight that the buttonholes squinted. And as I watched, an amazing thing happened. She started out plump, then sweater by sweater, blouse by blouse, skirt by skirt, she shrunk until she stood before me, a humped scrawny sparrow of a woman in a brown taffeta dress with glittery buttons.

I ran into the kitchen where my mother was stirring a pot of stew.

"Why me?" I screamed. Mother just shrugged and smiled, as if that were answer enough.

"Why me? Why not Claudia or Jennifer?"

"They're night owls, honey. Aunt Bessie's an early riser like you."

By the third day the battle lines were drawn. I divided the dresser. Lin-ing the mirror on my side was a row of eight dolls, which I dutifully dressed each morning, a three-tiered jewelry box that played "Around the World in Eighty Days," a cache of plastic pop beads and initial bracelets, a pair of clip-on earrings I was not yet allowed to wear, and a grainy five-by-seven of Ricky Nelson that I had scissored from *Teen Magazine*. On her side, under a yellowed doily, was everything she had unzipped from the satin pouch of her suitcase—a gold pocket watch, tweezers, a box of Polident, a framed picture of Lord Byron, a huge black purse with a clamp like an alligator's jaw, and a photograph of a sad young woman. My mother said it was Aunt Bessie's wedding picture, but I didn't believe her. I had seen plenty of wedding pictures—the bride radiant in a flouncy veil and pearls, her white-toothed groom bending over her as they cut the cake together, hand over hand, grinning into the camera.

No, I decided, the woman in this picture could not possibly be a bride. She was standing alone in a shapeless gown. Her head was bare, her hair yanked into a knot—not the silky chignon the women in *Wagon Train* wore, just a tight thin knot, without ribbon or other adornment. She was turned sideways, her head bent low, and she was holding—not a bridal bouquet with streamers—but one rose, drooping as if it were falling from her hand. My mother assured me there *had* been a husband and that he loved Aunt Bessie so much he built her a home in Stockwell, Indiana, with an oval window embedded in the front door, a home filled with beautiful things, like linen napkins pressed just so in the drawer of a heavy chest that stood in the entry hall. I didn't believe that either. "If Aunt Bessie was really married," I said, "where are the grandchildren?"

"She had one baby," my mother answered. "But it died a long time ago, long before I was born." I could not imagine history that ancient.

By the third week I was wishing Aunt Bessie dead, or at least transported to my sisters' room. I hated her oldness—the swish of taffeta down the hall, the clonk of heavy heels, and the mechanical clack of her loose dentures. Over the years many dentists had tried, but Aunt Bessie had a crooked jaw, and when my father finally located a specialist and paid hundreds of dollars for two sets that actually fit, she lost them both— one in a field in Pennsylvania, where we'd stopped to pick blackberries, and one at sixty miles per hour, in the cubicle bathroom of a Greyhound bus. Finally, in desperation, my father settled for an economy set. Every night I'd pull the covers over my head and try to sleep as she propped up a pillow, turned on the night-light attached to the headboard, and clacked her way through *National Geographic,* Browning's "My Last Duchess," seed catalogs, fairy tales, detective magazines, *Reader's Digest,* whatever she could find. She always ended with Byron. She didn't read silently with her eyes like normal people, but she didn't exactly read aloud either. She simply moved her crooked jaw a little and whispered, just enough movement to set her dentures clacking. That was the last sound I heard at night.

And in the morning I'd wake to the fizz of Polident in a glass by the bed. I'd look up through bleary eyes for my first sight of the day—Aunt Bessie leaning at the waist and pouring her powdery breasts into a stiff brassiere. She'd stand by the mirror and pluck a stray whisker from her chin. This disturbed me: a woman with whiskers. And not only whiskers. All over her body, hair sprouted in unlikely places—from her nostrils, her ears—migrating from the places where I judged it should be, the places where it was just beginning on me. She never shaved her legs, yet they were as smooth as the legs of a rubber doll. The pits of her underarms were hairless. Even her eyebrows were missing. She'd sketch them in each morning with a small black pencil that she kept rolled in a hankie. "Old maid," I'd hiss beneath the covers. Then when she was gone, swishing down the hall, I'd crawl from bed and dress for school, where girls with real eyebrows were gathering in the halls.

I had long since given up my dolls, but every Sunday I volunteered to dress Aunt Bessie for church. She was the only grown-up small enough and old enough to be under my control. Looking back, I wonder why she let me use her. Maybe she liked the attention. Maybe the feel of young hands was so comforting that she bore the humiliation.

I started with her hair. It was gray, but not the silver floss of my grandmother or the spongy blue-gray of widows whose hair is constructed each Saturday morning. Hers was the muddied gray of leftover snow. She'd lean over the kitchen sink, and I'd lather up the Prell. Wet, her hair was fine as a baby's. Her scalp beneath my fingers was pink and exposed, and I could hardly stand to look at it. I'd squeeze the wet hair into a towel, then coerce a rat-tail comb through, making parts for the yellow rollers—a row down the center from her forehead to the nape of her neck. Then pin curls on each side, above her ears.

It was the year of dryer bonnets—my mother had gotten one for Christmas—so next she would be put under. I'd slide the plastic daisy bonnet onto Aunt Bessie's head, and it would fall toward her eyes, over the scratchings of what was left of her eyebrows, their shapely arches having long since swirled down the drain with the Prell. I'd set the timer for ten minutes. With each minute, her face reddened and chapped, and she talked louder and louder, as if it were *my* ears that were covered. When the timer went off, I unrolled the curlers one by one, and for a minute she was a Shirley Temple doll, the ringlets tight and shiny from the heat. Then the artistry, the teasing and back combing at the crown to give her the fullness I'd seen in *Ladies' Home Journal.* Then two curls on either side of her forehead, swirling inward like a ram's horns. "Cover your eyes!" I'd shout, and her hands would jump to her face while I sprayed Aqua Net until she choked and begged, "No more!" I'd pat her hair, shoot one final spray, and she would smile. A little blush on her cheeks, a little pink lipstick. She'd replace the eyebrows herself while I held the mirror.

Bessie's hands were strong and fearsome, her yellowed nails like talons curving in. The manicure was the final challenge: the taming of a wild thing. First, I clipped the thick nails, then filed them into ovals. I rubbed cream into her hands and fingers. Her skin was thin, stretched over knuckles knotty as roots, nothing left but bone and gristle. I'd choose Avon, some childish pink or coral, and begin painting the nails. Two coats. Blow on them to dry. Then the dress. The black crepe or the navy blue taffeta? Maybe the white blouse with a cameo pin. I chose for this Sunday a flowery chintz my mother had made—pale green with yellow zinnias and a ruffled lace collar. "Fine," she said, and I slipped the dress over her head, over the safety-pinned strap of her brassiere and past her crooked hip. I zipped up the back and she was done.

I grew three inches that year, sailing past Aunt Bessie's lopsided shoulders. The waistbands of my dresses rose; saddle shoes that were fine one afternoon pinched my toes the next morning. I was Alice in Wonderland, a fever dream pulsing out of control. It didn't surprise my mother. "Kids grow at night," she said matter-of-factly. "That's why they wake up hungry. It's hard work." One night I woke with excruciating pain in my calves, as if my legs were being stretched on a rack. I kicked off the covers and grabbed my knees, pulling my calves in close. The night-light switched on above my head, and Aunt Bessie sat up, turning her face toward me. She was a drawing pad sketch, a gesture, a jot, the mere suggestion of a face. Eyebrows, teeth, the hair-sprayed pouf of morning hair were missing.

She sighed a self-satisfied sigh, as if she'd been anticipating this moment all her life. "Growing pains," was all she said, yet even that was garbled, delivered, as it was, toothless. She creaked from her side of the bed and walked in semidarkness to my side. She rubbed her arthritic hands together. Carefully she folded back the covers and touched my shoulder, coaxing me to turn. Then she rummaged in the headboard shelf and I smelled wintergreen as she squeezed Bengay onto her hands.

Why I gave in so easily, I still don't know. In daylight she was the last person I wanted, the last person I would have imagined touching me. I could have called for my mother; she surely would have come. But I was helpless in the pain and confusion of this newest trick my body was playing, and Aunt Bessie's hands went right for the hurting place. They kneaded and rubbed and tamed the pulsing muscles of my calves. Her yellowed, knotted hands, the protruding veins, the fingernails I'd painted orange just that morning. She squeezed more ointment from the tube, warmed it between her palms, and began to rub my calves again. After a while, the pain stopped. My tears stopped. And for the moment, at least, I stopped growing.

I recently discovered in my parents' antique trunk a leather diary marked 1897. It is Aunt Bessie's diary. In it are recorded the small moments of her seventeenth year. The handwriting is as eccentric and unpredictable as she was, at times painstaking in its perfection, at other times scrawling and nearly illegible. There are entries of anger and self-pity, loneliness and disappointment, then sudden wild-geese flights of joy. She wishes for the words to come more easily. She longs for the power to express the sting of a sleigh ride, the red burn of sunset, the taste of oyster soup and apples. Usually she borrows the words of others, Longfellow and Byron mostly, only occasionally breaking into songs of her own, recalling the gleam of sun on a field "ridged with frost" or a sky "cloudless except for a few fleecy ones in the east." And as I read the diary, it begins to make sense—my hunger for words, my very choice of vocation. I want to thank her, but she is not here.

Independent Spirits

Last of the Line

BARBARA ADAMS

You have the family conceit
in the lift of the chin
beneath the smileless grin—
I don't need anyone.

Here you are in bed for good
losing your mind,
finding it now and then
to recall a grudge, stoke a feud.

Childless, you tell me
how to bring up my kids—
you'd have raised (you're sure)
nothing but Nobel Prize winners.

You put me in your will,
giving me the key to your solo world—
bone china for twelve
with the dust of three decades, a cold bed.

Your life smells of mothballs
from your mother's closets,
clothes never worn turning black and dull,
like family love or silver.

You have the family eyes—
opals tinged with pewter.

It's all that's left of you now,
all I can see of my father.

Like him, you bear the family curse—
a stingy heart
that gave love by the drop
to one dying of thirst.

Aunt Moe Gets Reborn

DENNIS DONOGHUE

When I'm told someone acted out of character, I'm never quite sure what to think. Look hard enough, and you can usually figure out why a person behaves a certain way. No decision, it seems to me, comes completely out of the blue. Then I think of my aunt Moe.

Not long ago if you walked into her kitchen you'd find clean laundry heaped on the microwave, breakfast dishes stacked in the sink, and black smudges streaking the linoleum. You'd also find my uncle Eddie dying on a cot in the pantry.

"His tongue is a razor," she'd say. "Still."

I would sit at the table and drink instant coffee, my sympathy split between my skin-and-bones uncle and my godmother, who brought him tomato soup and saltines only to have the tray shoved back at her. She'd roll her blue eyes. I'd shrug. We'd talk about the weather, my kids, the old neighborhood—as if Uncle Eddie wasn't there.

"Moe's marriage is like the Boston marathon," my mother said once. "Early on it was bearable, but then came Heartbreak Hill, and she's been on it ever since."

Twenty years ago Uncle Eddie left the post office on a vague disability claim and spent his days drinking sixteen-ounce cans of Narragansett beer. A delivery truck would pull up onto the sidewalk on Fridays, and the driver would bump a half-dozen cases up the stairs on his last stop of the week. One day I arrived at the same time and lifted the blade of the hand truck over the top step while he opened the storm door. I stacked the cases in the back hall under a row of brass coat hooks.

"His world spanned a ten-foot radius," she told me. "Kitchen, toilet, cot."

A month after Uncle Eddie's funeral and three weeks after her knee surgery, Aunt Moe and I spent the morning hunting for a headstone. At Finian's she picked at her food, then left the table to use the bathroom. She didn't realize she was in the men's room until she looked in the mirror and saw a man in a business suit standing before a urinal. She blamed her heart medication. She lifted her cane from the lip of the sink and hobbled to the exit, struggling with the weight of the door and nearly going down on the slick tile.

"I used the men's room," she announced as I counted out money for the check. "Order me another sea breeze."

I lit her cigarette. Her hand shook. The lack of color under her fingernails suggested she might soon occupy the space next to Uncle Eddie. But who could blame her for walking through the wrong door? She'd just buried her husband of forty-five years. At the funeral, she'd worn navy blue, not black. With the mouthful of words left to him, Uncle Eddie had told his son, Redmond, and daughter, Siobhan, he loved them and wished he'd been a better father.

But not a word for Aunt Moe—no good-bye, no take care, no turn out the lights after I'm gone. At first she laughed it off, claiming she'd have squeezed it out of him had he left her enough to squeeze. Later she said that if he hadn't been so pigheaded and had let the hospice people swab his mouth, it would have been a different story.

"Are you okay?" I asked. "Do you want Motrin or something?"

I felt ridiculous asking her if she wanted something to clear her head. For starters, I had nothing to give her. She carried her own drugs anyway. So I sat and watched her smoke as the waitress went for her drink.

"I'm fine," she said. "I need a decent night's sleep."

Aunt Moe's empty house made noises she hadn't heard before, sounds that kept her awake and listening most of the night. Redmond and Siobhan lived out of state and had their own lives now. What kind of mother would ask her children to get on an airplane these days unless she was sure she was dying?

Later, after I helped her up the front steps and into the screened porch, she led me into the parlor where Uncle Eddie's personal effects filled a half-dozen double-knotted plastic bags. The contents of each bag had been hand-printed on packing tape, the bags propped on the couch.

"Know anyone with a size twenty-six waist?" she asked me. "He shrunk to death inside the same white T-shirt and pair of gray sweatpants. Most of the clothes still have price tags."

I slung a bag of dress shoes and sneakers over my shoulder after hurling five other bags into the bed of my pickup.

"Here, take this." She stuffed a crumpled twenty into my pants pocket.

"The donation box is three hundred yards up the street," I protested.

Twice she pushed my arm away. She wouldn't hear of it, although in my pocket I already had a Swiss Army knife that never left the box it came in and his old Timex on a flexible band that she'd given me.

The following Sunday after mass, I pulled up to the front of the church and found her chatting with Father Nolan, the priest who had said Uncle Eddie's funeral mass and recited the final prayers over his grave.

Her hand rested on his forearm as he lowered his head to catch what she was saying above the passing traffic. He nodded, then turned his face toward her ear to speak. Small groups of parishioners lingered on the cement apron below the church steps. The warm air smelled of moist earth and running snowmelt.

Eventually, Aunt Moe would notice me, but seeing her engaged and animated—at one point she rested her cane against her leg and flapped her arms to imitate a chicken—made me feel as if she'd rounded a corner of sorts.

"Such a handsome man," she said as we bounced along in the truck. She enjoyed the view from the cab, the high perspective it offered. "What a shame."

I knew what she meant, though I'd never heard her speak that way about a priest. Her tone implied he should have known better, that if he'd glanced in a mirror before entering the priesthood, he would have had second thoughts.

Aunt Moe and my mother had grown up with Father Nolan. Like us, his people were Connamara Irish, which meant, technically speaking,

Dennis Donoghue

we had a priest in the family. On Christmas Eve he came to her open house and led us in a rendition of "God Rest Ye Merry Gentlemen." Tall and white-haired, he sang with his eyes closed, picturing, I imagined, himself at the manger in Bethlehem instead of in the middle of a kitchen packed with drunks. Aunt Moe called him Jimmy, and one year she snuck up behind his chair and fixed a pair of reindeer antlers on his head.

"Think of what he's missed." She cracked her window to let in some fresh air. "It's crossed his mind, believe me, though it's another thing to get him to admit it."

"He's a priest," I said. "It must get easier over time."

"It's not normal to deny yourself," she said, "especially if you've had a thing for women. Before the seminary he got around, let me tell you. No moss gathered on that stone."

My hands grew clammy on the wheel. The truth was, I didn't know how he'd done it either, and hearing about his life before he'd become a priest made me think about Aunt Moe's life before she had married Uncle Eddie, a life which, according to my mother, was one of endless nights and countless boyfriends.

"I could never ask Redmond and Siobhan this because they'd think I was a candidate for the loony bin," she continued, "but you think a person could end up in hell? I mean a place of torment for eternity?"

"I doubt it," I said. "Are you worried about Uncle Eddie?"

She shook her head.

"He made his bed," she said.

At a red light she looked across the intersection, then dug into her bag for a cigarette. "Free will? What about that?" she asked. "As long as what you do doesn't hurt anyone."

"You plan to rob a bank?"

"I could use the money."

"Free will, yeah, that's something I believe in. I could buy that. But do we do as we please and burden ourselves with guilt later on? Or do we spend our lives sticking to senseless rules so that we feel as if we've been led around by the nose?"

"Okay, right," she said, waving a hand, indicating I'd lost her.

"No, really," I said. "If there's something you want to do, do it, especially after what you've been through. You have no one to answer to."

"That's no excuse," she shot back. "It's not as if I'm owed something. I wouldn't act out of spite, just do something because I felt like it. I'd have to have a good reason and believe in my heart it was the right thing to do. And the right thing for the other party."

"What other party?"

"The other person."

"Who?"

"Father Nolan."

"Father Nolan?"

"I reached out to him a year ago. I was desperate. I had to do something. Eddie called him a medicine man and told him what to do with his voodoo. Can you imagine? But God knows Jimmy tried. He did his best. I needed him then. I still do."

"He's helping you deal with Uncle Eddie's death?"

"We play Scrabble," she said, ignoring my question.

A week later I went by to take her grocery shopping and found her on an aluminum ladder clawing leaves from the top of a downspout with a garden fork. She'd had a neighbor ratchet the ladder over the gutter. She wore a pair of blue jeans and a black elastic knee brace. I'd never seen her on a ladder before, but her life with Uncle Eddie had taught her to do jobs women usually left to men.

"The water pours over this gutter like Niagara Falls," she called down to me. Clumps of rotted leaves blotted the walk beside the house. I dug out a broom and shovel from the cellar and swept up the mess while she climbed down and went inside to gather her coupons and returnable bottles.

"Do you know that recliner Redmond bought me with all the gadgets and storage inside the arms for my crosswords and remotes?" she asked as we moved down the dairy aisle. "The vibrator screws up my pacemaker. Every time I switch it on I get this fluttering in my chest. Oh shit," she said, spinning the shopping cart around and wheeling it back toward the front of the store. "There's Eleanor Maffin. She works at the rectory."

I glanced over my shoulder. A stick of a woman reached above the deli case, pinched a number from the dispenser, and waved it over her head.

"So what?" I said.

"God forbid a man and woman exchange the time of day around her. It's headline news. One look at this shopping cart and I'm finished."

Aunt Moe poked her head down each aisle and at the checkout fumbled with her pocketbook. She asked for paper instead of plastic to hide her purchases. She walked on the other side of me as we exited the store to prevent Eleanor Maffin from catching a glimpse of her.

"That was close," she said as we turned out of the parking lot. "She's been a busybody since fourth grade."

"You're safe now," I said.

When I set the bags on the table, the kitchen was as clean as I'd ever seen it. The linoleum shone beneath the bright light fixture. Green cleanser her sponge had missed powdered the sink drain. A basket of plastic daisies sat on the microwave. She slid the groceries onto the top shelf of the refrigerator: a jar of cocktail sauce, a round tray of cooked shrimp, two lemons, a small tub of onion dip, a quart of orange juice. She stacked boxes of spaghetti, cans of tomato soup, and four bags of Chips Ahoy! cookies in the cabinet over the stove. Into the freezer she stuffed a couple of Lean Cuisines and a box of Eggos. She pulled out a bottle of Stoli's by the neck and tilted it.

"Damn it," she said. "I forgot to get one of these." She refused to let me pick one up for her. She'd get by without it. More than ever, she added, she had to keep her head on straight. Clouded judgment wasn't a luxury she could afford right now.

She asked me to stay for coffee but without her usual insistence. She limped around the kitchen, favoring her knee. She folded the paper bags and pulled a lint brush out of a utility drawer. I had a hunch she was expecting someone, so I told her one of my kids had a swimming lesson.

"Now that's something I've always regretted," she said as she ran the lint brush over her sleeves. "Your mother's a fish. I sink like a stone. But who says a person can't change? Who says you have to be the same old person day in and day out? People look at me and they think, 'Oh there goes poor Moe, doesn't your heart go out to her.' But I'll tell you, I wouldn't bank on that sentiment lasting much longer."

I recalled those words when my mother's phone call came a few weeks later.

"Guess who just called from a pay phone in Portland," she began. "That's Portland, as in Maine. And pay phone, as in untraceable."

"Who?" I asked.

"Are you sitting down? Your aunt Moe, that's who. And take a guess who she's with."

"Who?"

"Jimmy Nolan. That's Father Nolan. The two of them went on a trip."

"So?" I said.

"An overnight trip."

"That doesn't necessarily mean anything."

"She's selling the house. She has Siobhan in a panic. Redmond is beside himself. And don't think I don't know about the conversation the two of you had that Sunday, Mr. Do-As-You-Please. You tell your aunt to act on whatever mood strikes her? Is that supposed to be funny?"

"We talked about free will for about a minute," I said. "I voiced an opinion. I didn't intend it to be any more than that."

"The road to hell," my mother said.

I could picture her face, the look that indicated that all her hard work on me had been a waste of time, that I hadn't learned a thing in forty-seven years.

"Do I deserve this?" she asked.

Our conversation was going nowhere.

"That's my oven timer," she said. "I have to go."

"She's a grown woman," I added.

"She's my sister who's run off with a Catholic priest, a widow not in her right frame of mind. But I guess this is a revelation to you."

After we hung up I prepped for more phone calls. What did I know and when did I know it? I'd tell whoever called that Aunt Moe and Father Nolan were adults. They hadn't kidnapped anyone. For a moment I saw them as they drove along the coast of Maine in the parish

Dennis Donoghue

37

sedan, searching for a radio station that played the music they listened to as teenagers. Maybe my mother was right. Maybe Aunt Moe wasn't herself. She was needy and vulnerable and had fallen prey to impulse.

But then I recalled how sure-footed she'd looked that afternoon perched on the extension ladder, more confident and focused than I could ever remember seeing her, as she went about the task of scooping debris out of the gutter so that rainwater could flow freely again.

Eulogy for Auntie Mame

LISA BEATMAN

One hot and sultry August morn
in nineteen twenty-one, I think,
a second Singer girl was born,
she Charlestoned out all wet and pink.
Let's call her Mildred, Gramma said,
just look at her, a baby flapper,
but Baby was a true redhead,
and wailed before the doc could tap her:

Oy vey, that name is such a bore,
too old and dry, the kids will tease,
and I have so much life in store,
for God's sake, call me Mimi, please.
And sure enough, she got her way,
grew to be the willful daughter,
to her momma's great dismay,
Mimi never did what she had oughta.

Class cutup extraordinaire,
ripe for laughs, convention's traitor,
on yet another double-dare,
she ran away to join the the-ater
And there she found her life's true calling,
a spotlight hush, a bit of fame,
an audience enchantress, Daahling,
everybody's Auntie Mame.

Lisa Beatman

Famed for lavish Sunday brunches,
clown-strewn basement tête-à-têtes,
artsy chat 'mid celery crunches,
masks of tragicomedy.
Now she's gone, but not really,
as we gather in her behalf,
she's still giving advice quite freely,
Now don't forget to live, love, laugh!

No wallowing in tears and frowns,
even when you're sitting shiva,
celebrate, send in the clowns,
go on out and live a little!
So if you lie awake and wonder,
listening to distant thunder,
maybe it's God and Aunt Mimi's laughter,
splitting a gut in the great hereafter!

The Businesswoman

AMINA

Spending the night at my aunt El's house was the best thing about being twelve years old. Since El and her husband, Johnny, had no children of their own, she spoiled all her nieces and nephews. My aunt El also raised my half brother Chuck, whose mother died when he was ten years old. One summer, for whatever reason, I got to spend a great deal of time at El's. It meant staying up to watch Johnny Carson and having a late breakfast with El, who worked at home.

In the early 1960s, El had all the trappings of the aspiring black middle class. A two-story brick home with a manicured lawn, complete with plastic pink flamingos in the backyard and a concrete birdbath. Inside, their furniture was French provincial reproductions, custom covered in plastic. The floor was done in plush wall-to-wall carpeting with exquisite oriental rugs that El told me she inherited from a former employer, a wealthy Jewish woman whose house she once cleaned.

I could never picture El as a housekeeper because at home her sister, Bertha, did all the cleaning and most of the cooking. Bertha, who lived with El and Johnny, worked as a live-in maid and came home only Thursdays and Sundays. Her on-again, off-again boyfriend had dropped her off this Thursday morning, and she was cooking dinner early because it was also her beauty shop day.

"El, you should be shame keeping a child up till Johnny Carson go off," Bertha said, laughing. "You keeping hours like a madam." Bertha always said El didn't know her way around the kitchen because she's a businesswoman. I never knew what Bertha meant, but this Thursday I was soon to find out.

I stumbled upon the meaning quite by accident when El asked me to pull up the blue-and-pink rug in her bedroom and beat it on the clothesline in the backyard. As I pulled up the rug, I found stacks of money bundled together with a big red rubber band. "El, why is all this money here?" I asked. She chuckled as she rubbed Jergens lotion on her skin. "Oh my, Shal, I forgot that money was there; it's for Mr. Dominic."

"Mr. Dominic? Why is this money his?"

El put on her Bermuda shorts and sprayed herself with Estée Lauder Youth Dew. "It's for my numbers," she said. "Now hurry up and beat that rug so we can eat breakfast."

"What numbers do you mean?" I asked.

"Shal, we will talk about that later. Now get moving so Bertha can run the vacuum in here and then you can take a nice bubble bath so you can learn to help me."

I had no idea what kind of help El meant, but I was totally fascinated by the thought. She always paid you for helping, unlike her brother, my father, who felt work was something that you had to do and you should be glad to be of service.

As I carried the rug downstairs, I passed through the pale yellow sun porch off the kitchen, where Bertha was peeling cooled potatoes for potato salad.

In the backyard, all kinds of flowers were in full bloom. Red and yellow roses and white mums bordered the driveway, and in one corner of the huge yard, a small garden of tomatoes, collard greens, squash, green beans, and cabbage grew. The clothesline was stretched in another corner between an apple and a plum tree that would bear fruit for the preserves and pies that Bertha made on her days off. I threw the rug over the clothesline and beat it with the small broom that was kept in the yard for that purpose.

Soon Bertha called me to come inside and wash my hands for breakfast. The table on the sun porch had been set with flowered linen place mats and matching napkins. El never allowed plastic or paper on her table. My plate was filled with my favorite link sausages, fried apples cooked in sweet butter till the edges were crispy, and two slices of white toast, cut and smeared with butter and seedless strawberry preserves. Bertha prepared sweet orange juice that she squeezed using a citrus reamer and served seedless in goblets. El could not stand seeds in her juice, a habit she acquired from the lady who left her the fancy rugs.

El had a warm, nut-brown complexion that all my daddy's people had. She also had facial moles sprinkled like freckles over her face. All the adults were tall with what we kids called a jump-up booty, a behind that stuck out almost like a shelf. El wore her long, silky hair in a French roll with two smaller rolls on either side of her head and a pompadour on top. She was tall and sturdy with long, flat feet that were never in heels, always flats. In the summer, she wore flowered housedresses with leather flats or a coordinated Bermuda short outfit. For Sunday church services, El dressed in Lilli Ann knit suits with patent-leather flats. In winter, she brought out of storage the furs and matching hats, which were worn with tall leather boots. She always tucked a vibrant silk scarf inside her coat.

Bertha and El hardly looked like sisters. Bertha was a lighter shade of brown and quite plump. She wore her hair cut short, straightened hard, and curled tight. Bertha had the same facial moles and wore glasses. On workdays, Bertha dressed in a white or pink maid's uniform. And, to my dismay, she would roll her stockings down around her ankles like doughnuts. Bertha favored loose housedresses and never wore pants until I was much older. The sisters lived together until Bertha's death.

At breakfast, my lesson began. "Shal," El said, "you must not ever tell anyone outside the family about my numbers."

"Sure, El, what are numbers?" I asked.

"People have dreams that they look up in the 'Three Wise Men' or the 'Red Devil' books. In it, they find a number and play it with me. If that number comes out that day, they win money, depending on how much they played."

Although I did not understand, I did know that my father's number was 698 and the year before he hit it pretty good.

As I ate, Bertha finished the potato salad, which was the best because her potatoes never got mushy. She made it with sliced hard-boiled eggs and lots of paprika. Bertha also cut up three chickens, prepared cabbage, creamed corn, and sliced tomatoes and cucumbers in vinegar with red onions. Bertha would fry the chickens when she returned from Ida Mae's Beauty Salon, a twenty-minute bus ride from El's house. Bertha didn't drive like El, who drove a brand-new Chrysler New Yorker that Johnny traded in every three years.

"Do you want me to pick up something sweet after I leave the beauty shop?" Bertha asked before leaving.

"No, Bertha, Dominic will bring some of that Italian stuff that Shal likes so much," El said. My eyes and mouth watered with anticipation. I loved cannoli with its crunchy crust, the tiny chocolate chips, and the creamy filling. The cream puffs were good, too, but cannoli was my favorite.

Mr. Dominic was an odd figure because not many white people lived near El's house in Detroit. There were just a few old Jewish people who could not afford to move, my father told me. Mr. Dominic came by every Thursday around dinnertime. Usually he would bring a box of cannoli, cream puffs, or sometimes the best bread ever. On those Thursdays when Mr. Dominic came, I had my first slice of pizza, Genoa salami, and the greenest olive oil I ever saw.

After a quick bubble bath and a spritz of Jungle Gardenia, I dressed in a matching short set and bounded into El's room. She was sitting on the bed with the bundles of money before her. She said, "Okay, I want you to count the money and put it into bundles of one thousand."

I knew one thousand only from math class and had never ever thought of money like that. "Make sure all the tens, twenties, and fives are together and all facing the same way," she instructed. I counted the money as El told me.

She took several small booklets from a chest of drawers and sat by the window near a card table that was folded up when not in use. The white lace curtains revealed a window box filled with red and white impatiens. After about a half hour spent counting and listening to Motown music as well as songs by Aretha Franklin and Jackie Wilson on a transistor radio placed on top of a chest of drawers, I had completed my task. I had counted out ten stacks of bills that El counted again, and then bundled together with thick, red rubber bands. "Okay, now, Shal, how much money is here?"

I didn't need a pencil and paper; one thousand times ten is ten thousand. "El, we have ten thousand dollars."

"Yes, Shal, that's right." She went to the cedar hope chest and removed a wooden box, opened it, and took out a yellow envelope that held about ten small envelopes with various names on them.

Then the telephone rang and El invited the caller, Big Leroy, who worked afternoons at the plant, to come by.

"Hello, Miss El," he said. "I sure am glad I hit. You know ain't been no overtime, I knew 273 would come straight."

El handed Leroy an envelope, and he counted the money. I went to the kitchen to get a glass of the lemonade for Big Leroy. When I returned, Big Leroy was wiping his forehead with a plaid handkerchief that he took from the back pocket of his work uniform. He finished his lemonade, then got ready to leave.

Then my aunt answered the phone again for the first of many calls that afternoon as customers called to play their numbers with her. "Hello, Eora, girl; yes, you want to play 456, 902, and 553 straight?"

This went on for about three hours, always with El adding at the end, "Now, good luck to ya, baby." When a lull came, I asked El why she was so kind to people like Big Leroy.

"Big Leroy is one of my best customers, whenever he hits I get a little something, too. All folks deserve to be treated nice, and you always remember that," replied El, looking at me over the glasses that she wore whenever she read or wrote her numbers.

I kept myself busy reading and counting the hour until Dominic came with his treasures. The time crept on, and I kept turning over in my mind the events of the day and the words of Aunt El. The numbers game that my aunt was involved with offered hope to the poor people who placed bets. El was well liked among her customers because she paid winnings in a timely fashion and always paid the correct amount. But she was interested in appearances, so El joined a ladies' group at a church that knew nothing about her business.

And she shared her earnings with family members; helped with tuition, car notes, and other necessities. And she rewarded my report cards and good grades and book report recitations with money. Through her generosity, I was able to attend charm school, and she made sure to attend my dance recitals, musical concerts, and church programs. I financed my first European trip with a generous gift from El. Through the years, she supported all of my endeavors, and I never received an empty holiday card, even into adulthood.

Aunt Bertha's Potato Salad

6 medium potatoes cooked till fork tender and cooled completely (Do not overcook.
    Potatoes can be refrigerated overnight.)
4 hard-boiled eggs
¾ cup chopped sweet pickles
¾ cup chopped celery
½ cup chopped onion
1 cup real mayonnaise
1 tablespoon cider vinegar
1 tablespoon yellow mustard
Pinch of sugar
Salt and pepper to taste
Paprika for sprinkling on top

Cut potatoes into small chunks. Chop 3 of the eggs; reserve 1 and slice for garnish. Add potatoes, chopped eggs, chopped pickles, celery, and onion into mixing bowl. Add mayonnaise, vinegar, mustard, and sugar, and blend thoroughly. Add salt and pepper to taste. Transfer into serving bowl and arrange sliced egg and paprika on top.

Dragon Lady

DOROTHY BLACKCROW MACK

When I was small, Aunt Eva always sent me postcards with exotic foreign stamps. She came to visit every Thanksgiving when we set the
table with starched white linen napkins, stiff and crusty in the lap, and
too many forks. Cold droplets would ooze down the outside of the
water goblets onto the soft linen tablecloth, but I was not allowed to
dip my fingers into that cool puddle. I was to "drink my water, not play
with it."

Aunt Eva was the extra person at the table. She was flat and colorless
in a tan double-breasted suit with a peplum, and tan stockings and sensi-
ble tan shoes. But she wore no corset, as I discovered when I had to
share my four-poster double bed with her. I'd watch her undress. Aunt
Eva was thin, her body curved, not chunky like Mama and Grandma
Lee, who wore corsets, hair nets, and black, thick-heeled shoes that
could easily crush a kitten's paw as it tried to drink milk beneath the
kitchen sink. Aunt Eva preferred thonged sandals or plush slippers.

She didn't wear a nightgown, either, but silk lounge pajamas and a
brocaded dark blue kimono with red and yellow dragons running up and
down the edges. On the back of the kimono two scaly red-and-yellow
dragons faced each other, each with blazing eyes, fiery breaths mingling.
Their tails curled downward into a knot. I was mesmerized. I longed to
trace the embroidery with my fingernails. But the ferocious dragon eyes
kept me immobile. Secretly, I called Aunt Eva the Dragon Lady. She had
no lashes on her puffy right eyelid. It scared me—thick and fleshy, wrin-
kled and bulging in the middle. Grandma Lee said that was why Aunt
Eva became a schoolteacher and never married. She told me that when
Aunt Eva was my age, she caught scarlet fever, and when the fever
broke, her right eyelid was gone.

"Grandma, how could it just disappear?"

"It just did. In those days people were dying so fast, my mother was just relieved that Eva pulled through. We were lucky to find a surgeon who made her a new eyelid from skin from the inside of her arm."

Once I had to get up in the middle of the night, and in the faint moonlight, I could see that puffy eyelid closed all the way. I was still scared of it, even shut.

Grandma Lee always made me wear white cotton gloves to keep my hands clean and protected from the coal dust that drifted down in the gray summer air from the mills along the Monongahela River in Pittsburgh, where we lived. The gloves bound my fingers, and I could never feel the air, the sun, anything. But if I didn't put them on, I'd be left at home.

"Germs! That's why you wear them. See how dirty you would have gotten?" Grandma Lee said as she looked at my coal-dusted glove tips.

I didn't get germs from escalators or elevators or streetcars when we went downtown shopping, but on the way home I dusted door handles, banisters and grates, and streetcar windows with my white gloves.

Aunt Eva wore white gloves, too, and hers stayed white. Once she came into Grandma Lee's house without taking off her coat and hat, swept into the front parlor, and sat on the piano stool, pumping the pedals furiously, her white gloves resting on the keys, not missing a note.

She stopped abruptly and turned halfway around. She'd seen me with her terrible eyelid.

"What are you doing here?"

I was crouched in the forbidden front parlor, carefully prying the loose tiles around the false gas fireplace with my fingernails.

"Nothing," I said, staring at the magic piano keys that kept moving up and down by themselves. I couldn't look at her.

Then she laughed. "You've never seen a player piano before?"

"No," I said, easing the last loose tile back in place and standing up on top of them. "Mama won't let me touch it."

"Well, child, come and see how it plays itself!"

I was afraid to move off the tiles, but she spun around to the piano again, flicking a metal switch that stopped the keys. Maybe she hadn't noticed, I thought.

She slid open a little door in the piano. "See, here's where the rolls of paper go, and when they turn, the holes catch to make the different keys go up and down." Then she shut the panel. "Flick the switch and it plays automatically, like I was just doing. But it's more fun to pump the pedals. Then you can make the music go fast or slow."

She beckoned with a white-gloved hand. "Sit here." I obeyed. Then she pushed the stool in so I could reach the pedals.

At first the keys wheezed out notes, but then I got the hang of it. Whee! I was making music, lovely happy music. Faster and faster I pumped as the keys pounded out "It's a Long, Long Way to Tipperary."

Suddenly the parlor door opened, and Grandma Lee peeked in. "What's all that racket?" Then she saw us. "Oh, don't let her go so fast! And you! Slow down, or you'll break the piano!" Then the door closed.

"That's probably enough for today," Aunt Eva said, taking off her gloves and hat. She went into the dark hall and hung up her long camel-hair coat, returning with just her clutch purse. Reaching inside, she bent down toward me. I wasn't afraid of her anymore, so I opened my hand. "Have a nail file. It helps to pry things loose."

I could tell from the tone of their voices, their careful questions about her plans, that Mama and Grandma Lee felt sorry for Aunt Eva because she was an old maid and all alone. They made sure she wasn't left out at holidays or the family reunions held in red Ohio barns.

Yet I caught a different look on their faces sometimes, wistful and faraway as they fingered the postcards she sent me from China or Manchuria or Singapore or Ceylon or Siam. Sometimes they were in awe as they read faded news clippings of foreigners being "shanghaied" during the Boxer Rebellion in China in the 1920s while Aunt Eva had been there. I saw envy when she brought back exotic, exquisite presents that were mostly useless.

She had a steamer trunk, papered with stamped customs permits and dents from Shanghai in the steel corners. When she opened it, chiffon

Dorothy Blackcrow
Mack

49

dresses billowed out—the dresses were nubby yet swishy around her knees, not stiff and slippery like taffeta.

On the other side metal clamps held satin drawers in place, drawers bursting with souvenirs—pearls, silks, milk green jade, Ming vases, incense burners shaped like junks, tall porcelain dolls dressed in kimonos with wide red sashes, pleated fans painted with white cranes amid bamboo, sandalwood shells of soap, carved ivory compacts, jasmine perfume, slippery see-through scarves. And, for me, a teakwood box inlaid with mother-of-pearl.

During the summers when she wasn't cruising the Orient, Aunt Eva lived "free as an ostrich" at Chautauqua, New York, soaking up lectures on transcendentalism, the poetry of Emerson, and music—concerts every night by the lake, recitals every noon by the fountain. She rented a cottage for the season. When I was ten, she invited me to come for two weeks and play my violin in the children's orchestra.

I begged to go. Even though I was still afraid of Aunt Eva, I liked her better than Mama. It wasn't her oriental gifts or her fascinating stories. She answered my questions. And she kept my secret about the tiles. I also kept hers.

I could sense my mother's reluctance to let me go, perhaps envy, even though she didn't care for music. But I promised to practice, so I was sent by train, complete with baggage and instructions to behave.

I slept in a cot on the back screened porch. My little space had a cardboard dresser and a music stand and a metronome for practicing scales out there in the evenings. The porch was cool and private, surrounded by large catalpas and chestnuts. I loved sleeping outdoors with the birds and the rain, and if I lay very still, I could hear the waves lapping against the lake's shore.

Aunt Eva slept in the big four-poster with Geneve, her lady companion, who taught French at the same high school as Aunt Eva in Canton, Ohio. Over and over I whispered her name—like my birthplace, Geneva, New York—but with only two syllables that floated in the air. Geneve was young and exotic; she was part French and came from Quebec.

She had marcelled hair, like Aunt Eva's, but hers was cropped short in a bob and shaved close in the back like a man's, with a black curl at the nape of her neck. It was called a ducktail, but I saw it as the tip of a heart, coming to a point at the back of her round dark head.

My thick straight hair was parted in the middle. Aunt Eva would braid it every morning, unbraid it every evening, and brush it before my bedtime.

Aunt Eva's silver-blonde hair was wavy on the sides, wound tight in a high bun at the back. I never knew how long it was until one night she loosened her bun and her hair fell down to her knees in ripples. As Aunt Eva stood brushing my hair, Geneve found a silver hairbrush and began brushing and brushing Aunt Eva's hair, too, as our favorite opera singer Nellie Melba sang and sang on the Red Label record playing on the Victrola.

At bedtime Geneve wore the navy blue silk kimono with the red and yellow dragons. It was so beautiful, I wondered how Aunt Eva had given it away.

But if I was very careful, Geneve would let me wear it to play wedding with my new friend, Sarah, from New York City. Sarah played cello in my orchestra, and she stayed at a cottage three alleyways down. "Here comes the bride, all dressed in . . . red-and-yellow dragons!" We screamed and laughed as we ran down the hallway runner rug into the big cottage kitchen. We never tired of Dragon Lady weddings.

In the mornings Sarah and I played in the children's orchestra, and in the afternoons I practiced for my daily lesson with "the Maestro," a European first violinist from the Boston Philharmonic. Then Sarah and I could go swimming. How I loved the lake! No chlorine-filled YWCA pool with whistles and mandatory showers. In the late afternoons we would swim out to the raft and back.

One day in late summer Sarah and I swam all afternoon, then went to her cottage for blintzes—much better than peanut butter sandwiches—and played a new game called Monopoly. I lost track of time. Suddenly it was past dusk. Dark! Had I missed supper? I grabbed my swimsuit and towel, and ran through the alleyways to Aunt Eva's cottage.

Dorothy Blackcrow Mack

All the lights were on as Aunt Eva and Geneve waited for me on the front porch swing, rocking slowly in the cool twilight. Geneve was holding Aunt Eva's hands.

"Where have you been?" said Aunt Eva as she glared at me.

"I'm sorry. I forgot. We were playing—"

"Don't you have any sense of time?"

I hung back on the bottom porch step, dangling my wet towel and swimsuit in front of me.

"Can't you see the girl has no idea?" Geneve interrupted, standing up abruptly. "Here, I'm giving you my watch. It's Swiss and will keep good time. So you won't have any excuses for being late."

I saw Aunt Eva stare at her as she removed the silver band and slipped it on my wrist.

"Thank you, thank you, Geneve," I said as I turned on the threshold. "Now I won't ever be late again!"

"Hmmph." Aunt Eva said, rising stiffly from the porch swing. "Well, child, come in and eat. You must be starved." She held the screen door open for me. "We saved you some of your favorite peach cobbler."

Back home, Mama frowned. "So where'd you get the watch?" She didn't believe in frivolities, especially for young girls. The watch was ornate silver, old-fashioned with a big face, and unlike the postwar watches in the five-and-dime. I'd deciphered the worn script engraved on the back: Eva Shelton.

"I—uh, Aunt Eva gave it to me."

"Why?"

"I was late." Oops! Now Mama would really disapprove about my getting a present for misbehaving. But she let me keep it. Now I'd have no more excuses about coming home late from school.

Every summer I went to Chautauqua and played in the children's orchestra, then the youth orchestra until I left home on scholarship to study at the Paris Conservatory. Sarah, still my best friend, went to Juilliard. For my travels, Aunt Eva paid my airfare and gave me her Shanghai steamer trunk; I took it along, even though I had to pay extra for air cargo.

By then, Aunt Eva's hair had turned white, and she'd begun to use a teak cane, its head a carved ivory dragon. Geneve, still dark and beautiful in those old-fashioned chiffon dresses, would guide her arm on their early evening strolls.

How I remember those cool evenings by the lake, rocking in the porch swing and drinking mint tea from Ceylon! We ignored the gramophone's crackle as Nellie Melba and Galli-Curci poured liquid passion from their throats, lingering high C notes that floated on the air.

After Aunt Eva's death, Mama couldn't find the dragon kimono she wanted. I smiled, knowing it was still being worn in Canton, Ohio. Aunt Eva had already given me all that I'd ever needed—airfare, a Paris allowance, and her mother-of-pearl-inlay teakwood box. Inside is an old watch that no longer keeps time and a snapshot of two young women arm in arm, smart in their fringed flapper dresses, tipped cloche hats, and gloves, standing beside a steamer trunk on a wharf in front of the SS *Orient*. I see Aunt Eva's drooping right eyelid, still winking—right at the old metal nail file, which I still use to pry things loose.

Dorothy Blackcrow Mack

Growing Up in Irondale

ROGER CROTTY

My aunt Nonie grew up on the South Side of Chicago in a place called Irondale, a place that doesn't exist anymore. Irondale was always a little hard to pinpoint geographically. It was south of South Chicago, west of the East Side, right near South Deering. St. Patrick's, Trumbull Park, and Wisconsin Steel were the major landmarks.

Aunt Nonie was not a small woman. In fact, she was just the opposite, an imposing figure. Her attire had the same qualities: checks, plaids, big flowers in loud colors, great sparkling pins, dangly clip-on earrings and necklaces with beads the size of the marbles that we called boulders. Aunt Nonie, I'm sure, never read the fashion tips on what a woman of her size should wear. I don't think she would have paid any attention, anyway. She didn't want to hide anything about herself. To me, she was perpetually cheerful, with a sincere but loud laugh. And she could really tell a story.

Whenever she got together with my father and her two sisters, the conversation would eventually drift back to days gone by. We'd say, "They're back in Irondale again." When I listened to their stories, Irondale became real; I defined it more as a time than a place. They grew up in an Irish enclave, with lots of people who had the same or similar last names. So nicknames were used to distinguish one O'Brien from another or one O'Connell from another. I can remember hearing stories about Cocky O'Brien: Wasn't he a stuck-up character? Served him right when he married that Maureen what's-her-name. Or Dry Hair Linnehan, didn't he work for the city? Or Dingbat Fennel, who nearly lost a leg under a streetcar.

As they reminisced about people from Irondale, Aunt Nonie had a litmus test that she applied to each of them. When her mother died, there was the usual two-night Irish wake at Brown's Funeral Home. Like at all wakes, there was a register to sign when you visited the funeral parlor, and Aunt Nonie had the register memorized. Whenever a name would come up in the conversation, she would comment either "she came to Ma's wake" or the devastating "she didn't come to Ma's wake." That comment colored a lot of what was said afterward.

Growing up, Aunt Nonie lived with her mother, sister, and brother (my father) at 9919 Exchange. The other member of the household was a dog named Puddles (because he made a lot of them). Every afternoon there was a minor explosion when the three kids came home and threw wood, kerosene, and a match into the stove. This always made the neighbors downstairs fear for their lives. St. Patrick's Church and its school was a major factor in everyone's life in Irondale. The nuns at St. Patrick's all seemed to have strange names like Sister Irenez and said things like "Pray to St. Rock; he'll help you with your math." My grandmother worked at St. Patrick's; that's how the tuition got paid, sometimes a little late.

In Irondale people went to dances held in the field house in Trumbull Park. Those dances were one way my family used to remember people in their neighborhood. If they couldn't remember someone, the first question was always: Did he or she go to dances? Aunt Nonie, who was nicknamed Smiles, definitely went to the dances and was considered quite a catch. Old pictures of Aunt Nonie attest to the fact that she was an attractive young woman. But teenagers in Irondale didn't have time to worry about dating or pimples. They were expected to go to work. And Aunt Nonie worked for the telephone company for more than forty years, retiring in her fifties. She spent most of those years working in the south Chicago office where she was the assistant chief operator. She later worked in the Englewood office as the night chief operator. Aunt Nonie was the first in our family to make it into the management ranks—not bad for a woman who left grammar school at St. Patrick's for a job at the phone company.

Another factor that kept Aunt Nonie single was that she was the child who cared for my grandmother her whole life, not an unusual role for a young woman in an Irish family. She took good care of my grandmother, something that wasn't always a walk in the park. During my lifetime, my grandmother was in her sixties and seventies. By that time she was tired mentally and physically. Her husband died, leaving her with three children under ten at home, and she had to go to work to put food on the table. My grandmother had severe arthritis, and I remembered all the weird remedies she was always trying to relieve her pain. After sitting at home by herself all day she was often in unpleasant humor when Aunt Nonie arrived home after a full day's work. In fact, the reason Aunt Nonie took a night job at Englewood in her last years of work was so she could be home during the day with my grandmother. Aunt Nonie accepted what life brought her, always cheerful and giving, and that made a big impression on me.

Aunt Nonie's life revolved around Irondale, the phone company, and taking care of Ma. They both lived with us until I was in fifth or sixth grade. They slept in a bed with short slats that sometimes worked away from the frame, sending Aunt Nonie and Ma crashing to the floor in the middle of the night floor, along with the springs and mattress. My father once tried screwing the slats to the frame, but that didn't work. I don't know why they never bought slats that were the right length.

Friday afternoons with Aunt Nonie were special. When I was about four, we would walk down to South Chicago Avenue and catch the number 5 streetcar. We got off at Eighty-eighth to stop at the phone company so Aunt Nonie could pick up her weekly paycheck. We always talked to her boss, Miss Macintosh, and went to the second floor, where operators answered calls, saying, "Number please," and plugging long cords into holes on the switchboards in front of them. Most of the ladies would say "Hello, Miss Crotty" to my aunt, and they all told me what a good-looking boy I was.

We then walked to SS Peter and Paul to go to Novena. I can still feel, see, and smell that church today. It smelled of Catholic churches, of incense and old leather. It was a wondrous place for a left-handed (religiously speaking) Irish/Swedish kid who was to become a Lutheran.

The highlight of our afternoon was going to Commercial Avenue. The three blocks from Ninetieth to Ninety-third and Commercial were to our neighborhood what the Strand or Broadway are to other places. There were three dime stores on Commercial: Scotts, Kresges, and Woolworth's. Every Friday Aunt Nonie bought me something in one of those wondrous places, usually a ball. She also bought me gliders, paddleballs, and yo-yos. Aunt Nonie always let me get the expensive yo-yos, the 15-25 centers, and the ones that "stuck" so you could make them do wondrous tricks, like whistling.

For Christmas or my birthday, Aunt Nonie usually got me an article of clothing. But she never got the right size—everything was always too big. I think that was because she thought of me as bigger—in size, word, and deed—than I really was. And when I was with her, I felt that way, too.

Eventually Aunt Nonie and my grandmother moved to a flat on Seventy-ninth between Langley and Evans. After they moved, we would go to the Capitol Theater on a Friday night. The Capitol had two things to recommend it: It was one of the few theaters that got first-run movies direct from the downtown theaters, and there was a great hamburger place next door. Even now, I can taste their hamburgers served with a big onion slice and accompanied by a chocolate shake.

After Ma died, Aunt Nonie and her sister, who was widowed by then, moved to Ninety-third and Oglesby. They would occasionally get obscene phone calls. But Aunt Nonie had a solution. She bought a whistle—the kind that basketball referees use so players can hear them when twenty-one thousand fans are screaming at the United Center—and she would blow it when the person on the line started his whispering act.

The alley next to their house was sometimes used by lovers who would park their cars there late at night. Aunt Nonie discouraged them by waiting for a crucial moment, throwing open the back door, and hollering for all to hear, "Why don't you go rent a motel room?"

Although Aunt Nonie never married, she had her share of gentlemen callers, those willing to brave the looks and comments from a mother who looked on these men as threats to her security. Aunt Nonie sometimes got tickets for White Sox games from one particular gentleman friend named Joe, or from her best friend, Mrs. Sullivan. At one game, Aunt Nonie, my brother, and I had box seats right behind third base. I thought I had died and gone to heaven. Those trips with Aunt Nonie most likely made me a lifelong Sox fan.

When I graduated from college, Aunt Nonie was there for the cele-

Roger Crotty

bration. The evening before the ceremony, my roommates and their families joined our family for dinner at a local Italian restaurant. Aunt Nonie, dressed in her finery, ate everything served to her, whereas the refined North Shore fathers with their tender tummies requested hamburgers. After dinner, we went to a Drama Club play. The moment the lights dimmed, Aunt Nonie fell fast asleep. The next day when I received my diploma, Aunt Nonie was there. I had no problem finding her in the crowd. Her hat, a true masterpiece, was the kind that made me wonder how she held her head up under all that weight. Later, back at the dorm, my roommates rolled their eyes as they referred to "your aunt Nonie." I refrained doing the same about their fathers, but, in my heart, I admired my aunt for being 100 percent herself, no matter what the circumstances.

The last time I saw Aunt Nonie was a Friday. When I walked into the hospital room and saw her, I knew that it would be the last time. During the hour I was there, sometimes Aunt Nonie was alert and sometimes she wasn't. One time she called me by my father's name, Jack. And she asked whether Ma had called to tell me that she had left last Sunday. It must have been one of those times when living with my grandmother was a little difficult. She told me she wanted my wife and daughter to have some of her jewelry after she was gone. Aunt Nonie loved her collection of jewelry. She thanked me for coming to see her. And as she always did, she asked how work was going. I told her that my family was eating regularly, and she said that was all that was important.

The moment that I will always remember was when I told Aunt Nonie that we were going to the Sox game on Saturday. Aunt Nonie told us to have fun. Then she started complaining about how "all you hear about is the Cubs." Here she was on her deathbed and she's mad because, like all of us enlightened South Side Sox fans know, in Chicago "all you hear about is the Cubs."

It's how I want to remember Aunt Nonie. In my life, I have always been surrounded by women who are giving people. My life has been enriched by all of them—Aunt Nonie was one of the first. And I imagine I got from Aunt Nonie the gift of storytelling.

Aunt Nonie wasn't a saint. She was a human being, shaped by her times. I guess, like my grandmother, she was sometimes hard to get along with. In her last few years she may have decided it was her turn to take it easy while other people took care of her, like she had taken care of Ma all those years.

Still, she was my aunt Nonie, and I love her and I miss her. When the phone rings late on Sunday afternoons, I always think it's going to be her calling like she often did. But it won't be her because she's gone. They're all gone now. Aunt Nonie was the last one. Maybe she's back in Irondale.

Roger Crotty

Tia Sonia

BEVERLY JAMES

I awoke after a dream-filled night that left me tossing and turning and swatting mosquitoes in my tia Sonia's one-level brick house in the coastal town of Tela, Honduras. I stumbled from the cot in the extra bedroom, a room actually the size of my closet back in the United States. But it had everything I needed: a rectangular wooden box on which stood a hurricane lamp, a crude drawing of a blond, blue-eyed Jesus, and a chamber pot. Sunlight flooded the room as I rose, swiping away the damp, hot sheets that clung to my legs. Rubbing the sleep out of my eyes, I pushed aside the plain cotton cloth nailed in front of the window and peered out at the rooster crowing on the neighbor's roof. Tia's house was considered quite impressive in Honduras. While most houses in this small town hugging the Caribbean Sea were wooden shacks with dirt floors, Tia's brick house had wood floors, a semiworking bathroom, and running water. It even had a carport, though Tia has never owned a car.

I could hear Tia in the kitchen, chopping and stirring food for the day's meals. Though seven of her eight children had left home, she still cooked enough for hordes of people. I made a quick trip to the bathroom, then followed the smell of refried beans and fried plantain to the kitchen. A breeze from two open windows wilted under the heat coming from the stove. Tia was boiling green bananas in a pot and baking tortillas in a pan. The rough, wooden table that dominated the center of the room was crammed corner to corner with goat cheese, *pastelitos de carne*, refried beans, sliced avocado, and a steaming pot of *mondongo*, or pig tripe. I told Tia my dream as I scooped up beans and chunks of meat with a hot tortilla.

I had fallen asleep clutching my ex's picture to my chest, feeling more regret and loss than I thought one heart should have to sustain. He had agreed to see me one last time before my trip to Honduras, but only to reiterate that, no, there was no chance of our getting back together. He had met someone new. That was five days ago.

"That man gonna leave you," Tia Sonia said as she bent over a scarred piece of wood that she used to knead tortillas. "That man already got somebody, and he gonna leave you, so ya might as well start lookin'." Lifting a beefy arm to wipe away beads of sweat, Tia tilted her head to see my reaction. I just shrugged my shoulders and walked over to the window. Her words were a waste, because he had already walked out of my life. I pretended to swat flies away so she wouldn't see the tears welling up in my eyes. But she knew; Tia knew everything.

"No use cryin' for no man that don't want you, you know. Fa true he gonna leave her, too."

I knew she was right. Tia Sonia had always been right. *La bruja,* the witch, that's what everyone in the family called her. Ever since I tore at cotton diapers stuck to my plump bottom in Honduras's sweltering heat, my tia had made the occult her calling. She never tried to hide it; in fact, she boasted of her fortune-telling skills.

"*La gente,* they line up outside my door to see me," she bragged. "They know I can tell them whatever they lookin' for. *Fijate,* who else gonna tell dem what true?"

My mother and her sisters back in the States would cringe every time someone who had visited Tela would relate the news that my tia still made her fortune with candles, tarot cards, and bones. Five of the six sisters and all three brothers would send money to their sister back in Honduras, hoping to change her way of life into something more respectable. Not my mother. "It's one thing to smoke somebody out," my mother explained, "it's another to make a living doing that."

My mother and the other tias would routinely get together in someone's basement to smoke cigars and chant to get an unsuspecting victim to do their will. It never seemed to work, though they claimed success wherever they could. "You tink you Tio Albert woulda marry Tia Joann? Not until we smoke him out, *mamita.*" To my mother and her sisters, a quiet smoke, scratching names in a black candle, all of that could be handled discreetly. But to hang up a sign and advertise for business, well, that was too much.

My mother was the only one who didn't send money to Tia Sonia. That parasite, blood-sucking leech. All names my mother spat out every time one of the tias would call to remind her of her obligation to the only sister left behind. No, my mother would not support Sonia while she made a living as a witch. "Extend a helping hand, and she gnawin' on ya goddamn elbow," my mother complained.

But Tia Sonia always did things her way. Sonia was the lone holdout when it came time to find a new life in the United States. Everyone else packed up their tattered chinos, cotton shirts, and worn dresses for the trip. They understood that life would be better in America. Not Tia Sonia. And in her own way, she was right. Business was booming in Tela. Lots of folks wanted to know whose husband was cheating, who poisoned the neighbor's dog, when the next child would be born.

Tia would always ask me to serve *café con leche* while she prepared diligently for her visitors. The parlor, the largest room in the house, was polished and swept clean. She removed the white cotton cloths from the windows and replaced them with heavy, brown drapes. Tia lit black and white candles around the room and set them on two round mahogany tables that gleamed with carvings of her gods—like the sun god, who seemed to leer at visitors, or the fertility god, who holds an ear of corn in front of his unnaturally erect penis.

Tia placed a steel folding chair at either table before she began her readings. Clients waited in the carport playing dice or card games like pitty-pat until she called them in one at a time. I always expected Tia Sonia to sail into the parlor wearing a turban and a colorful getup. Instead, she would come in refreshed after a long bath, powdered and cool in a cotton shift just tight enough to hug her hips but loose enough to let a breeze cool her heavy butterscotch-colored breasts.

Funny, I've never been afraid of going into that room. I don't believe my tia's gods have power over me. Maybe I've allowed myself to believe that my Westernized religion protects me from her hateful little demons. As she dispensed advice to the lovelorn and desperately poor, I was lulled by the soft sound of her voice. I loved to hear her stories of love gone wrong, of men duped by women who were unsure who fathered their babies. My mother hated these visits, cautioning me that in time Sonia would reap the punishment reserved for those who chose obeah as a full-time profession.

I stayed with Tia Sonia only a week, returning home to tend to my child, who never wanted to visit Honduras and see abject poverty up that close. Back home in bed, soothed by the sound of my daughter's soft grunts as she slept beside me, I instinctively clutched my chest as I reached to hush the ringing phone. My mother was on the other end: her predictions for Tia Sonia had come true.

My cousin Roycito became angry that Sonia wouldn't continue to fund his cocaine habit. He begged his mother for a few *lempiras*, concocting a story that he needed the money for a ride to La Ceiba. Tia Sonia called him a liar, walked into her bedroom, and locked the door. Roycito, my mother said, climbed up on the roof and broke into his mother's bedroom through the ceiling. He hacked her eighteen times with the machete Tia used to chop open coconuts, splattering the walls and furniture with her blood. His pregnant sister, stopping by for a visit, heard a moan and peered into the bedroom window expecting to see her mother with her latest lover. She locked eyes with Roycito, his hands dripping crimson, his mother's blood falling in dewy globs from jewelry he snatched from her dresser. She ran to the neighbor's house. He ran and ran.

My mother was the only one who refused to return home for the funeral. "Not me, *fijate* he could come after me." Caught by the police, Roycito had already managed to escape and find solace at his woman's house. Seems if you're crazy enough in Honduras, the police leave you alone.

I always wondered why Tia didn't predict her own grisly demise. And I will always wonder if death is the price for carving out your own path. Was she a pioneering entrepreneur, as I like to see her? Or was she the devil my mother delighted in calling her? Sometimes when I hear news from someone who has recently visited home, I clutch my heart and think of my tia. "Life is short," she always said, "so live it, sweetheart. Live it like ya gonna die tomorrow."

Beverly James

63

A Troublemaker Tells Secrets

JEFFREY HIGA

It is an immutable law of families that the person the adults hate the most, the kids love the best. In our family, that person was Aunt Elizabeth. As my mother's oldest sister, she was an unavoidable fixture at family Thanksgiving dinners, although not at the de rigueur Christmas dinners, an absence she explained to me as, "More than once a year? No one is *that* thankful for family."

As far as our parents were concerned, once a year was enough for them also, because Aunt Elizabeth was the worst kind of troublemaker: a teller of secrets. She refused to speak to us as children, and willingly went into the gruesome details about the horrors lurking in our family closet. For our parents, that single transgression, her refusal to pretend that we were a perfect family, was reason enough for their hate.

But to us, Aunt Elizabeth was the most grown-up person we knew. She was pretty, a fact that even my mother conceded. "Yeah, pretty like the serpent in the Garden of Eden." Aunt Elizabeth was raised in that generation in which a woman never went outside without a hat, and she was the only woman in our family who wore high heels all the time, leaving our mothers to their flats. She also smoked like a movie star, continuously and elegantly, using long black holders, to avoid smearing lipstick on the cigarette, which she found vulgar.

Like many great personalities, she spoke of herself in the third person, a tendency I discovered one Thanksgiving when I was six, when I took her my favorite board game. She looked down at me, arched her perfectly plucked eyebrow, and said, "No one has explained it to you, have they?"

I shook my head.

"Aunt Elizabeth doesn't do that crap," she said. "She doesn't play Chutes and Ladders."

She paused to blow smoke in my face. "You understand?"

I nodded my head. "Aunt Elizabeth is no fun."

"That's right, good boy," she said, patting my head like a puppy just learning a new trick. "That's why I like you best."

Being her favorite afforded me no special favors, no preferential treatment. And as far as I could tell, being her favorite was a pure accident of birth. Aunt Elizabeth always visited her siblings whenever one of them had a child, not to share in the joy of the parents but to judge what she considered the future of her lineage. It seems that she came away disappointed each time till I was born, when she is reputed to have laughed as soon as she saw me a few days after my birth.

"Look at this face, he looks like a little Dalai Lama," she said, picking me up. "This one has a very old soul."

She held me up so she could laugh at my face some more.

"You can have all the others," she told the other family members in attendance. "This one is good. I like this one."

My mother tells me that the other parents never forgave her for that. Despite this, however, Aunt Elizabeth was our savior. Whenever she was in attendance, we kids could become as unruly and disruptive as we wanted because any anger that was directed at us would pale against the ire Aunt Elizabeth could inspire. She was hated for her acerbic tongue and bright intellect, which churned out unstinting criticism of everything she turned her mind to. In the narrow window of time between her late arrival and early departure from Thanksgiving dinner, she always managed to infuriate every adult member of the family. Sometimes the anger would bubble up through old grudges, like the Thanksgiving Uncle Harry accidentally set too many place settings at the table, which prompted Aunt Elizabeth to comment, "The man can't count. Is it any wonder he lost his business?" Many times, however, she took Thanksgiving as an opportunity to create wounds afresh, like the time she pointed across the table to Uncle Tony's new wife and asked him, "What else besides her boob job do you two have in common?"

As a result, no one else seems to remember Aunt Elizabeth with the

Jeffrey Higa

fondness that I do. After Thanksgiving dinner, I could hardly wait until Aunt Elizabeth had her last cocktail and left, so that the reviews could come rolling in: "Oh, that was terrible what she said to Steve. I've never seen him so angry," or "You know, I have half a will to call that Elizabeth up and give her a piece of my mind. The nerve of her to say that." Family secrets and shames that were never spoken about would come pouring out then, illuminated by everyone's angry invective and indignation at Aunt Elizabeth. Allied against a common enemy, those after-Thanksgiving dinner conversations were lively and vibrant, and not the poor excuse for after-dinner conversations we have now about college bowl scores and how we all ate too much.

The only sign of their affection for Aunt Elizabeth was the sympathy they showed her by never mentioning her failed marriages. Although sure-footed in other aspects of her life, Aunt Elizabeth was unlucky in love. She had been married and divorced so many times that few of us are able to remember any of her husbands in particular, only the melancholy air and the nervous glances they all seemed to have in common.

Since men were unreliable income, Aunt Elizabeth owned what my mother uncharitably called a "junk shop" on the piers of Honolulu. The store catered to tourists and locals alike; its success lay in the fact that both groups were physically separated from each other. The front part of the store was for tourists, where it underwent several transformations to meet the needs of her eclectic clientele. In the 1960s, it was a head shop, selling paraphernalia to the hippies. In the 1970s, she imported ethnic goods like kimonos, saris, crystals, and African jewelry. In the 1980s, Aunt Elizabeth made it into an army-navy surplus store, selling East German army hats and insignias before the fall of the Berlin Wall. Through the years, she sold the opihi shellfish, limu seaweed, and octopus that the old fishermen would bring her, as well as surplus sailing through the store's unmarked back door. The old salts would come bearing gifts of seafood, poke among the shelves of junk in the back room, and chat up Aunt Elizabeth, bewitched by her aloof attitude, short skirts, and high heels.

By the end she was left with only her family to visit and care for her in the hospital. My aunt remained her old contentious self, and, after a couple of visits, most of our family stopped going to see her except my mother and me. In one of our final visits together, I asked Aunt Elizabeth why she remained so grouchy. She rolled her eyes, exhaled loudly, and gave me the derisive look that recalled my childhood.

"Well, honey," she said, emphasizing the endearment she had never used with me, "they won't let me smoke in here *and* I'm sober."

Aunt Elizabeth has moved from this life to the realm of myth. Whereas other families can refer to their epochs by births, deaths, or graduations, our family shows their belated affection for Aunt Elizabeth by recalling family events that she inspired, such as the year that Aunt Harriet burst a blood vessel in her eye because she got so mad when Elizabeth put out her cigarette in Harriet's awful pecan pie, or "the Thanksgiving Uncle Steve was so mad at Aunt Elizabeth that he couldn't see straight, and he missed the garage and drove his car into the side of the house."

And now this, the year that I acted just like that troublemaker Aunt Elizabeth, and told our family secrets to everyone who can read.

Jeffrey Higa

The Mystery Writer

M. J. ROSE

When I came home from school that afternoon, the door to my parents' bedroom was closed, which meant my mother was on the phone and didn't want to be disturbed.

Instead of going to the kitchen to get a snack or to my room to do my homework, I assumed the position. Sitting down, legs crossed, back against the bookshelves that lined the hallway outside of my parents' room, ear pressed up against the four-paneled door.

At first, I heard only crying. Soft gentle sobs. My skin prickled, and my heart started to pump. My mother was not a crier. I had not ever seen her weep. But I cried enough to know what it sounded like. I held my breath and waited.

Who was she talking to? There was no way of knowing until she started talking again. And she wasn't speaking at all. Just listening. We were all good listeners in my family, my mother often said. "Too good," she teased when she found out that I'd been at it again.

I don't remember when or why I started listening in on my mother's phone calls. There were not great secrets in our house. She usually shut the door when she was talking to her girlfriends or her mother, or one of my aunts, because, she told me, it was unnerving to have me sit and watch her when she was on the phone. But I was always worried that there were plans afoot that I needed to know about.

"You can't," I finally heard my mother say in a shaky voice that was sadder than I'd ever heard her speak before. I was picturing her in the pale pink bedroom, feet up, sitting against the soft pillows, phone up to her ear, looking out the window.

A long silence ensued, during which I figured my mother was listen-

ing. It was boring when she listened, and usually I read the book titles
on the shelves surrounding me during the long pauses.

The Fountainhead.

From Here to Eternity.

Lost Horizon.

Inside the Third Reich.

The Naked and the Dead.

The Old Man and . . .

She had started talking again.

"There are other solutions. Barbara, please. Just listen to me. There
are other solutions."

She was talking to my aunt. My father's middle sister. A smart and
savvy woman who worked as a buyer for a department store in Chicago.
I didn't know her well. We lived in New York. Mostly we only saw her,
my uncle Simon, and their son and daughter at important family gatherings. My grandparents' fiftieth wedding anniversary. My cousin's bar
mitzvah. I pictured her but could only remember that she was taller
than my mother, painfully thin, and always wore a very noisy charm
bracelet that caught on my hair every time she hugged me.

"You are not too old and you both make enough money to hire
someone to help. Barbara, listen to me. You can't do this."

For Chanukah, Aunt Barbara always sent my sister and me extrava-
gant gifts from the store: fur muffs, cashmere sweaters, velvet skirts.
You always wanted to touch the things that she sent, not just wear
them. There was a sensuous feel to what she picked out. To how she
dressed, too, though at the time I wasn't consciously aware of it. But
her necklines were always a little lower, and her dresses were always
a little shorter, and her heels a little higher than anyone else at those
parties.

"No." My mother was almost shouting now, the sorrow replaced by
anger.

I'd never heard my mother talk to anyone like that, other than my
sister or me or our father. It was an intimate anger. I knew how her face
looked now that she was so mad.

In the silences while my mother was listening to what my aunt was

M. J. Rose

69

saying, I tried to imagine what they could be talking about that would make my mother sad and angry at the same time?

Death.

It had to be. Someone in our family had died, I knew it. One of my father's parents? But why would that make my mother angry? I tried to think, angry and sad? When had I felt those two emotions at the same time? When my father punished me for being mean to my sister. Was Aunt Barbara yelling at my mother for something she had done? It wasn't possible. What could my mother have done to my aunt?

It was hot in the hallway. And I was hungry. Lunch at school that day had been soggy chicken à la king; white and thick and tasteless. I hadn't eaten any of it. I imagined that there was chocolate pudding in the refrigerator and thought of how smooth and cool it would be. But if I got up to go get it, I might miss some piece of information that would explain the conversation. So as ravenous as I was and as much as I wanted something—if not chocolate pudding, then peanut butter and jelly on crackers, or a glass of strawberry-flavored milk—I knew I was going to stay in the hallway, listening.

Sometimes when my mother kidded me about listening all the time, she segued into how that would make me a writer. "One day you are going to write down everything you have ever heard us say into a book, aren't you?"

She was convinced that when I grew up I was going to be an author. And I didn't mind her fantasy. I loved reading. I especially loved when she read to me. Or when we read the same book and talked about the story over dinner. Sometimes when we finished a book, we would invent what happened after the book was over. What would the characters do next?

We didn't have to do that with my favorite books, though. There were over thirty Nancy Drew books, and each one continued her story. I had read twelve of them so far. And each month, my mother took me to the big Doubleday bookstore on Fifth Avenue and Fifty-seventh Street and bought me one more. She had read the girl detective stories herself when she was growing up, and there was something so special about reading the books she had read.

I thought it would be a good thing to be a writer when I got older.

But it would be even better to be a detective like Nancy Drew and solve mysteries with as much success as she had. Well, here was a mystery, happening in my very own house. And I knew if I listened hard enough and paid attention, I might get the clues I needed to figure it out.

The first clue was that it had to be something very big for my mother to be upset like this. Especially because she was talking to one of my father's sisters, and she didn't even like her that much. Even then, at eleven, I knew that my mother was not close to the people in my father's family in the same way that she was close to her own friends or her family. His sisters were selfish, I'd heard her say to him. They thought only about themselves and never went out of their way for anyone else unless there was something in it for them. He'd disagreed, bringing up those gifts my sister and I got, and my mother had countered that it was no big deal for her to send them: she was the buyer for the children's department. And besides, she had to do it.

The spines of the books were hurting my back, the floor was cold, and I needed more clues. The one-sided conversation was not yielding enough information. In order to figure out what was going on, I needed to hear more than a one-sided conversation.

Getting up and moving as quietly as I could, I walked down the hall and into the kitchen where, very, very gently, I lifted the phone off the receiver.

I was absolutely forbidden to do this and had gotten in trouble more than once for listening in. I'd been lectured about why it was wrong and punished severely, but I was betting that my mother was too upset to hear the faint click of the receiver being picked up.

There was a trick to picking up the phone so that the person on the end couldn't hear. You didn't just lift it up . . . you started to lift and then when you got just a little space in there you stuck your finger on the plastic tab and kept it down until the phone was in position up against your ear and then v-e-r-y slowly lifted your finger up. It was almost foolproof. Especially if you were practiced at it. At the same time you clamped your hand down over the mouthpiece so the person on the other end could not hear your breathing.

I did all that and then, breathless, and proud of my stealth, I waited.

"Irene, it's a mistake. I am not having it. I didn't call you to talk me

71

out of it. Or to approve. I'm asking you to come with me. We'll say we are going to a spa. It will only be three days. Dick won't mind. And you have Judy there for the kids."

"No."

"I can't believe this. How dare you take the high road."

"I've had three miscarriages. I had to take drugs to keep from having more."

"What does that have to do with this? I don't want this baby," my aunt said.

"You just think that. When you have it and hold it, you'll feel differently. It's just now, the unexpectedness of it, the idea of starting over that has you spooked."

"No I've had enough of raising children. This is my time now. The kids are in school all day; I don't have to feel guilty when I go to work. You don't work; you don't understand the conflict. And I am not asking you to. I just need someone who Simon knows to go with me. He's so fucking suspicious anyway."

"I'll take it," my mother said. She wasn't really listening to what my aunt was saying. "Dick and I will adopt the baby."

Standing in the kitchen, listening to their adult conversation, I was getting more and more frightened. What were they talking about? Was Aunt Barbara going to have a baby she didn't want? Was my mother going to bring it here? And what would my uncle be suspicious about? And how did you get rid of a baby, anyway? Adoption? But that didn't make sense. She wanted my mother to take a trip with her and lie about something. That didn't sound like putting a baby up for adoption. Besides, she was saying she didn't want to go through another pregnancy.

In 1964, eleven-year-old Jewish girls who lived in New York City and went to private school knew a lot about reproduction but not much about sex or drugs, rock and roll, or illegal abortions. Very little about the conversation made sense to me.

"So you won't help me?" my aunt finally asked in a weary voice.

"Please have the baby."

"Oh, Irene, grow up. It's not even Simon's. You want to adopt a baby that I had with some salesman from Texas?"

Silence. My mother said nothing. My aunt said nothing. I wonder now if she was sorry that she had told my mother that last part, but I never found out because after that my aunt just said "thanks" in a sarcastic voice and hung up the phone.

That night at dinner I tried to think of some way I could find out the details of what they had been talking about, but I didn't know what to say that wouldn't give away the fact that I had heard almost all the conversation. I waited to hear if my mother was going to tell my father anything about the phone call, but if she did it wasn't that night in front of my sister and me around the dinner table.

How do you get rid of a baby? It obsessed me. Interrupted me from doing my homework; stopped me from enjoying the *Honeymooners* that night on television.

I asked my friends the next day in school, and we conjectured about how people might throw babies away, and why they would throw them away. If they weren't married, if they were poor and couldn't feed them. If they just didn't want them because they were monsters.

Finally, at the end of the day, I got caught up in a Brownies meeting, then a rehearsal for a play we were doing for school, and then my grandmother picked me up at school with her dog, whom we took to Central Park; by that night, I'd lost interest in my aunt and her dilemma.

Several years later, my father's father died, and we went to the funeral. It was sad but not the way it is when someone young dies unexpectedly. My grandfather was eighty-six and had battled diabetes for years. He death was not unexpected, and the event was more nostalgic than it was wrenching.

What I remember was my aunt Barbara—still too thin and very lovely dressed in a black designer suit—coming over to my mother and kissing her hello. My mother moved back just a few inches so that my aunt's kiss didn't land on her cheek but in the air. Her voice was chilly when she said hello, and she managed suddenly to notice that my sister was fighting with another cousin and so had to go over to end the argument right away.

I followed my mother as she walked across the chapel to intervene. After she had pulled the two cousins apart, my mother said she wanted to go outside and asked if I wanted to go with her. It was hot in the funeral chapel, she said. But I suspected that my mother, who was never

M. J. Rose

73

that close to anyone in my father's family, wanted to get away from them for a few minutes.

We stood on the porch of the funeral home and saw my aunt leaning against her car in the parking lot, smoking a cigarette.

The whole conversation came back to me. I was sitting in the hallway again, hearing my mother crying, feeling hungry, then going into the kitchen and listening to those scary words about getting rid of the baby.

"She had an abortion, didn't she?" I asked.

My mother nodded. "How did you know?"

I didn't answer right away. My mother frowned, and then smiled ruefully. She was remembering something. "You listened?"

I nodded.

"How old were you? Nine? Ten?"

"Eleven," I said.

"Too young," my mother responded. "I wanted to take the baby," she said.

"I know."

"One day you're going to write about it, aren't you?"

I smiled. "Why do you always say that?"

"Because I know you."

"I could never write about it."

"Why?"

"Aunt Barbara would be too upset if I did."

She thought about that for a beat.

"Fuck her," said my mother—who cursed very judiciously—and then she took my hand and we went back inside.

Tropical Aunts

ENID SHOMER

Aunt Debs and Aunt Ava. They were my father's sisters. Dramatic, glamorous women, who my mother said had "been around." I saw them every July when we traded the humidity of Washington, D.C., for the even more oppressive heat of Miami, where my father's people lived amid piña coladas, guava jelly, and floral-print clothing. I still have a picture of them mounted in one of those plastic telescopes that were popular key chain trinkets in the 1950s. They looked tan and healthy and non-Jewish standing arm in arm in front of the cardboard palm trees.

Debs was the older, a stormy, rich blonde who had been widowed. She lived a reclusive life in a houseboat on the Miami River. Without a phone, she could be contacted only through her attorney, like a movie star. Ava was a redhead with a reputation for borrowing money. Everyone knew she'd had to get married to her first husband. This was the biggest scandal so far in our family. After she had the baby, she got divorced, lost custody, and married an osteopath who worked nights as a stand-up comic in the hotels of Miami Beach.

My Florida aunts came north to visit us only twice. The first time was for my sister Fran's wedding. They drove up together in a big white Chrysler sedan. "My teeth started to chatter as soon as we hit North Carolina," Aunt Debs said, hugging herself as she closed the car door. She regarded our snow-covered lawn as if it were the surface of the moon. Then she picked her way slowly up the front walk. Ava followed, relatively sure-footed in doeskin loafers and thick white socks. She leaned down to touch the snow shoveled into a heap alongside the front stoop and put a drop of it on her tongue. Just like that! "Sometimes we put Hershey's syrup on it and make snow cones," I told her. When I saw her eating snow so impulsively, I understood how she could have gotten pregnant.

As soon as they had hung up their clothes, they unveiled the presents: for my mother, a white lace bathing suit cover-up; for my father, a book called *Fish of the Southern Waters*. My gift was a pearly-pink comb-and-brush set with shells and sea horses embedded in the handles. For Fran, they'd chosen salmon-colored lingerie that made my father blush as my sister eagerly held it up for us to admire. "Baby dolls," Aunt Ava explained. "I hope your Herb will like them."

The night before the Florida aunts arrived my mother had briefed my sister and me. "Don't mention Uncle Teddy," she cautioned. Teddy was Aunt Debs's dead husband.

My father, within earshot in his lounger, pitched in. "Did you put away the liquor?" Fran and I looked at each other. The only time my parents drank was at Passover, when they sipped reluctantly at four glasses of Manischewitz Concord wine. Beer had never crossed our threshold.

"All I have is the bottle of schnapps," my mother said. She was talking about my grandfather Velvel's bottle, which she kept on hand for him the way you'd keep medicine for an asthma attack.

"Are we supposed to pretend Uncle Teddy never existed or what?" Fran asked.

"She took his death so hard," my mother said. "Just avoid the subject if you can."

I remembered when Great-uncle Benny died. The whole family mourned for a week at my aunt Florence's house, where the gilt mirrors were covered with black cloth and the satin love seats crowded out by low, uncomfortable wooden folding chairs.

"Aunt Debs must have really been in love," I said, looking at my sister and remembering an old movie about a girl whose fiancé was killed on the way to the wedding. Would Fran turn to drink if Herb were killed after the final head count had been given to the caterer?

"Teddy was a charmer," my mother said. "Could charm the birds out of the trees."

My father lit a Lucky Strike. "That girl really suffered when he went. I even had to hide the scissors."

This explained, at last, my father's prolonged visit to Florida the autumn before. My parents had flown down for the funeral, but my father had stayed an extra three weeks. At the time he had said he was helping Aunt Debs settle Uncle Teddy's estate. Now my imagination ran wild with scenes in which my aunt Debs, her large blue eyes reddened by grief and alcohol, was saved from self-destruction by my father, who in my experience had not been up to dealing with bloody knees or temper tantrums.

Later that evening I persuaded Fran to let me into her room. She was setting her hair. I eyed the birch bedroom set and pink clock radio, the wallpaper with its primroses and small yellow birds. As soon as Fran was married I'd be moving in. I smeared some of her Dippity-Do on my hair.

"Your bangs will look like sheet metal if you use that much," she said through a mouthful of bobby pins.

"Who do you like best, Aunt Ava, Aunt Debs, or Aunt Florence?"

"You must be joking. Ava and Debs treat us like their own kids."

"Mom says they spoil us rotten."

"That's because they don't see us often," Fran said.

"I wish Aunt Florence would move to Alaska," I said. Aunt Florence was our mother's brother's wife, a stout woman later diagnosed as diabetic whose bleached-blonde hair was done up in a zillion curls like a telephone cord on top of her head. She referred to her kids as "my Maury" and "my Melissa," even if they were standing next to her. I was jealous of and hated both these cousins. "I'm glad you're getting married before Melissa," I said.

"Melissa's a bit young to be thinking of marriage," Fran said from her great tower of eighteen years. Melissa was sixteen.

"Aunt Ava eloped when she was sixteen." *Eloped* was the word everybody in our family used for her shotgun wedding.

"Aunt Ava's different," Fran said as she opened the door and gestured me through it. "You can't talk about her and Melissa in the same breath."

Fran was right. The Florida aunts were different. Aunt Ava was a model, but not the kind who strolls down runways or appears on the cover of *Vogue*. Her portfolio was full of magazine ads for shoes, gloves, detergent, and jewelry. She had supplied the hands and feet. "A perfect size seven B," she'd say, pointing her toe. "And feet don't show age like a face does."

Aunt Debs had kept her husband's accounts. "They weren't ordinary books," my father had told my mother last fall after Uncle Teddy died.

"Well, when he had the dry goods stores, the books were just a little irregular now and then. But after the deal in Las Vegas?" His voice had trailed off to a low, knowing snicker.

At the wedding the two sides of our family would have a chance to get to know one another better, my mother said at breakfast the next day. The Florida aunts were still asleep.

The northern half of my family—my mother's side—had always acted superior to the Florida half. It had nothing to do with pedigrees—they were all immigrants from Russia, Poland, Hungary, and Romania. I think now it was envy, for the northern relatives vacationed in Florida for two weeks each winter and talked of retiring there to a life of golf, sunshine, and shrimp cocktails. For them, Florida meant relaxation. Anyone who lived there year-round had chosen good weather over hard work. My father had told me at least a thousand times that I wasn't a Yankee like them. This was confusing coming on the heels of my mother's pleas that I attend Hebrew school and join the Young Judea group at my junior high. Would they need to know if I was a northern or southern Jew?

My father's family had left Baltimore's harbor district in the early 1920s, part of the Florida land boom. My father spoke of this period with such reverence that as a very young child I pictured them in covered wagons, carrying rifles and beef jerky. My grandmother Minerva opened a beauty shop in Lemon City, claimed to have invented the permanent wave before Nestlé, and dropped dead of heart failure at the pari-mutuel window when I was four. She and her children took to the tropical landscape without a hitch. They ate hearts of palm; gambled on dogs, horses, and jai alai; and carried fishing tackle at all times in the trunks of their cars. Though my father claimed that the aunts spoke

Yiddish just like my mother's side of the family, I'd never heard a word of it pass their lips in eleven summers in Miami. They had picked up *un poquito Español*, which, Ava said, came in handy on weekends in Havana.

"I want to sit with the aunts at the wedding," I told my mother.

"Out of the question. We've already discussed it."

"It's my sister getting married," I argued. I looked at the wall calendar: the red circle that represented Fran's wedding loomed at me like an angry eye. The entire month of December was full of arrows, asterisks, and my mother's notes. If I ever married, I'd elope to Elkton, Maryland, just for spite.

On the day of the wedding, Debs and Ava included me in their beauty rituals: eyebrow tweezing, oatmeal facials, hair setting, leg waxing, manicuring, and eyelash curling. Much of this was new to me because my mother, a size twenty, spent her cosmetic energy experimenting with corsets and girdles. She paid little attention to her face. She used no foundation but blotted her shiny freckled face with a puff dipped in light rachel powder. The lipstick was applied the way you'd put a dash in a sentence.

Finally, after six hours of primping, we dressed. Debs wore a green satin sheath that emphasized how slim she was—without dieting, my mother said. Ava was startling in a silver-sequined dress that fell from her body like enchanted water. I stepped out the door in my red French heel pumps as if I were wearing someone else's body, one that was fragile and required stiff posture so as not to smudge the makeup and hair.

At the reception, I had to eat with Maury and Melissa, but after dessert Debs and Ava invited me to their table. Debs was a little drunk. She leaned on her elbow, chin in hand, drawling and cooing like a pigeon. Ava spent much of the night on the dance floor, sometimes dancing alone. The light bounced off her silver dress as she twirled and dipped. At eleven o'clock Fran tossed her bouquet—right through Aunt Debs's arms and onto the floor. Debs stumbled trying to pick it up but managed not to fall.

After the wedding my mother relaxed, went off her diet, and spent a week playing card games with the aunts while a record snowstorm buried the capital city. She ignored the donor luncheon she was organizing for the synagogue where she was president of the sisterhood and where the rest of us set foot only for the high holidays.

Looking back now, I think she didn't approve of the Florida aunts. If they had been men, she'd have had no trouble appreciating their guts and eccentricities. But as women they must have frightened her. They had survived hurricanes. They had moved alone through nightclubs, funeral parlors, divorce courts, and casinos.

Under their influence, my mother recollected her girlhood. "When I was fourteen, I had a blue silk matching coat and dress that cost $200," she told Aunt Debs. She turned to me to explain. "That was when you could buy a dress for $6.95."

"Hen," Aunt Debs said, taking the pack in a canasta game, "you wouldn't believe some of the getups I've seen in Vegas."

"Not in your wildest dreams," Ava added. She had visited Debs and Teddy at the casino. "It's hard to tell the hookers from the rest of the crowd."

"Hookers?" I asked.

"Whores," Debs explained.

"Please watch what you say." My mother glanced at me.

"I'm old enough to hear," I protested.

"I'll decide that," my mother said.

"Teddy knew everybody," Debs said, without a hint of wistfulness. This remark was met with silence by my mother and Ava.

"Even Frank Sinatra?" I asked.

"Sure. You want to know something about Frank Sinatra?" I nodded. "He still calls his mother every day. Just to check in."

They talked, too, about long-dead relatives who figured in the family mythology, praising the pioneer spirit, which had brought them out of the hopeless bondage of Eastern Europe and onto the shores of America.

"You know you're part Gypsy, don't you?" Aunt Ava asked me suddenly.

We were playing rummy in teams—my mother and I against the aunts. "Gypsies?" my mother and I repeated.

"Our grandfather's father was a Gypsy, a stable hand for a branch of the royal Romanian family," Ava explained.

"Really?" I asked, my mind already full of campfires, gold hoop earrings, and colorful skirts.

"Absolutely," Debs said, stubbing out a cigarette and lighting another.

"I never heard that one," my mother said.

Aunt Debs cupped my chin in her free hand. "That's why you're so dark. Like your great-great-grandfather."

"Come on," my mother protested. "There are no Jewish Gypsies." Her laughter was met with silence.

"Hen, we wouldn't kid about a family thing," Debs said. "He worked in the stables, taking care of the horses. And the riding boots."

"Riding boots?" My mother's voice sounded for a second like Eleanor Roosevelt's, shaky and high-pitched.

Ava elbowed me. "If you ever get the urge to roam, you'll know where it comes from."

I knew it had to be true. I could already feel the Gypsy blood in my veins. It had always been there. It was the reason I didn't want to join Young Judea. I couldn't belong to any group.

"He must have converted," my mother said, still puzzling out loud.

After the aunts left, I moved into Fran's room. The wallpaper with its birds and flowers reminded me of the house we had rented the year before in Miami, with its hibiscus bushes and iridescent hummingbirds. But we didn't go to Florida the following summer. My parents sent me, instead, to a Jewish camp in the Poconos, where I stumbled through transliterations of blessings and songs and sneaked out at night to smoke with the boys. I didn't see the aunts again for eleven years.

Debs continued to live in seclusion on her houseboat. She became involved with the Humane Society, gave up meat, and adopted a variety of dogs and cats. Ava gave up Judaism for the teachings of an Indian avatar named Meher Baba. When I was fifteen, she sent us a photograph of him with his finger to his lips. Her letter explained that he'd taken a vow of silence more than twenty years before and that she was going to India to live in an ashram with his followers.

I wasn't too surprised to learn in the mid-1960s that Ava and her husband had moved to a religious commune near Orlando and that Debs, who'd been hitting the bottle again, had joined them.

. . .

After Fran married, she moved into a split-level home ten minutes from my parents and had four children in quick succession. I tried not to hold it against her that my parents never complained about her, that she was their idea of a model daughter. My own interactions with my parents over the following years went like this:

"Have you met any nice boys lately? What about that boy Maury introduced you to? Is he going to college?"

"What boy?"

"Maury's friend."

"Maury who?"

"Your aunt Florence thinks you should go to college here in town. What's wrong with George Washington University?"

"It's here in town."

"She hates me. My own daughter hates me."

My brilliant report cards failed to impress them. In my mother's eyes, I was valuable cargo waiting to be unloaded. Then her marriage mode would set in: invitations, napkins and matchbook covers with embossed hearts and my name intertwined with the name of someone nice, someone they approved of, someone Jewish. Caterer. Photographer. Bridesmaids' gowns. Dyed silk pumps. And me, dressed up in white, an offering to the God my mother served at her donor luncheons.

At last I graduated from high school and won a scholarship to a New England college, a Yankee after all, my father complained. I didn't come home for the summers. After college, I went to Europe for a year. I threaded my way across the continent on a Eurail pass, picked grapes in Italy, and worked as a secretary in London. I pictured my relatives speaking of me the way they used to speak of the Florida branch— with a slightly disapproving air.

It was a beautiful fall day when I retrieved my mother's letter from general delivery in Edinburgh, where I was visiting. General delivery was the only address I used that whole year; it gave me the illusion that I might never settle down, that I was beyond the reach of family. The letter was marked URGENT and explained that Fran was sick. It ended with a plea for me to telephone immediately.

"She had a tumor on her spine," my mother said when I reached her. "They removed it," she whispered. "It was malignant."

The word *cancer* filled my mind, fiddler crabs with their pincers up-raised like the ones I'd chased every summer as a child along Biscayne Bay. I tried to imagine Fran with a life-threatening disease but could only produce the image of her with baby after baby in the maternity ward of the hospital. "Will she be all right?"

"I waited to write you, hoping to have good news. She's had radia-tion and all her hair fell out. She weighs eighty-six pounds."

I remember looking through the window at the heather that purpled the September fields, wondering if it grew anywhere else in the world. Everybody was pitching in, my mother said. Herb, though, was falling apart. Could I come home and take care of the kids? I could sleep in the guest room in the basement. I flew home the next day. In my mother's voice there had been a music that caught me up in its melody, its refrain. We can save her, it said, if we try hard enough.

But we couldn't save Fran, and my mother, who lived all her life conserv-atively as a kind of white magic against tragedy, was beyond consola-tion. My father called in the Florida aunts toward the end of Fran's illness. They stayed at Fran's with me, sleeping on cots in the rec room. They cooked, cleaned, and baby-sat with a fervor I wouldn't have ex-pected. But even they, with their perpetual Florida tans and tropical ra-diance, were lost in that swaying throng of mourners dressed in black.

The funeral was held in the poshly appointed Zimmerman's Star of David, the largest Jewish establishment in town. I had never experi-enced grief before, and now I used it as an excuse to avoid Melissa, Maury, and the rest of the Washington clan. I held on to my sacrifice like a shield and refused to cry through the rabbi's long eulogy, waiting for the grief to hit me like a tidal wave, for it to grab me like a claw.

At the cemetery, a snow-covered hillside in Virginia, my parents fainted and were helped back to their feet by the Florida aunts. My aunts Debs and Ava were everywhere, consoling the family, lending a hand when the awning threatened to blow down at the graveside, help-ing mourners in and out of cars. They wept freely, not for themselves, Debs confided to me in the limousine, but on my parents' behalf. Ava

Enid Shomer

was more silent than I had remembered her. She had a silver streak through her hair—whether natural or peroxided—like Indira Gandhi. It gave her an otherworldly look, like a badge of wisdom obtained at great expense. "There are no rewards for us here," she said at the grave. Her green eyes swept the horizon.

After the burial came the shiva, the week of mourning. Zimmerman's had delivered to Fran's house a dozen wooden chairs small enough to be elementary school furniture. When we returned from the burial, my aunts dutifully unfolded them, then served the platters that friends had sent. Only the immediate family had to sit in the little chairs, terribly uncomfortable on purpose to keep the mourners' attention on pain and grief. The aunts brought us food and encouraged us to eat. During all of this service they were as humble and quiet as geishas.

The eating and crying continued until the last guest left and my sister's husband, Herb, collapsed into sleep. Finally, only my parents, the aunts, and I remained. Ava suggested my mother relax on the sofa. My mother, mutely obeyed, moving in a daze. She removed her shoes and stretched out the length of the couch. "God," she suddenly said. "I helped Frannie choose this fabric." She felt the nubby tweed of it and sobbed. "What's the point?" she asked us all.

"Oh, Hen, I'm so sorry," Ava said.

"I know," my mother said.

"But Hen," Ava continued, "there's something I want to tell you. Something you have to know."

All of us looked at her.

"She isn't really dead," Ava announced. I could hear the sound of jubilation and conviction in her voice. "No one dies. We all come back. I knew it when I was in India. You mustn't think of her as lost forever."

My mother looked to Aunt Debs.

"Yes," Debs agreed. "Somewhere your Fran and my Teddy go on. Transformed." She exhaled. We watched the smoke hang in the air like a magician's rope trick.

My mother bolted upright on the couch. "You're crazy!" she shouted. "Both of you."

"No, Hen, you don't understand—"

"You've always been crazy. Only now you call it religion. We're leaving. Get our coats," she ordered my father.

"Please," Aunt Debs begged, tears streaming from her eyes.

"Wait, Ma," I called to her as she punched her fists through her coat sleeves.

"Wait for what?" My mother turned to me with the same venom she felt for the aunts. "My Frannie's dead. Who cares if she comes back as something else? She isn't coming back to those four children. Or," she socked her chest, "to me."

That was the last time she ever saw the aunts, though she and my father eventually retired to Florida. The aunts tried to contact her, but she dismissed all apologies and returned their letters unopened. And I think, mild as she was, that she took pride in having taken so absolute a stand against them. She refused to speak their names. She tended this anger like a garden, nourishing it on the anniversary of Fran's death. Fifteen years later, home for a visit, I watched her light the yahrzeit candle and heard her say, "Back as a flame? Only a little flame?"

The aunts left the day after the funeral. I knew I'd want to defend them if their names ever came up, if I ever found myself sorting through the family mythology. And I knew I'd never change my mother's mind about the incident. She needed that anger too much. I could imagine myself far into the future, living in Taos or San Francisco, some place I'd never been, talking to a child with a face I couldn't picture clearly, a dark face like mine. I'd tell her about the wedding—not my own, but Fran's.

When their plane taxied down the runway I wished I were with them, our faces leaning in a threesome toward the small window, the city spreading out below us like a game board. The trip south would have felt like walking under a very large shade tree, a tree so large that the coolness under its branches went on and on into nightfall.

Enid Shomer

The Gutter Gals

JANICE J. HEISS

I could never understand why my dad's sisters, Daisy and Lilly, spent every minute together despite driving each other nuts. When I was a teen in the 1950s, it was an adventure to spend a weekend at my cousin Sally's in Skokie, Illinois. Seeing my aunts in action was high drama, electrifying and revolting. I had never known anyone remotely like them, and I never knew how to take them. Were they really as bad as they acted? Aunt Daisy, the meaner, more hard-bitten of the two, resembled a comic-book character; she couldn't be real, could she? Was it all just an act? Who's kidding who? as my aunts used to say. But I had to take them seriously. After all, they were family. My cousin Sally said her mom, Daisy, was born mean. Was this possible? Was it in my genes also? I wanted to find out, yet I feared it, too.

One visit during summer vacation in 1958 sticks like flypaper on my mind. Every day, my aunts met at one or the other's duplex at eleven A.M. for their third cup of coffee. They lived a block from each other in matching nondescript units, and were the first duplex owners in Skokie to incorporate Astroturf on the floors inside and out. Skokie and my aunts seemed halfway around the world from where I lived, just forty miles away in the suburb of Rivendell, with its stately colonial homes and spacious two- and three-car garages.

Sally and I stayed in her bedroom until we heard the doorbell ring and knew it was safe to come out as we weren't allowed to talk to them before their third cup. Who would want to? Aunt Daisy woke up spitfire mean and scary-looking, her mouth all caved in without her false teeth. Minus her teeth, she talked as if possessed, with the sound seeming to come out of a hidden orifice.

Sally and I didn't mind being holed up in her bedroom as we gabbed and gabbed about our crazy family. Living closer to all my relatives, Sally knew a lot more than I did. She told me that Grandma Isabelle threw fits and banged her head against the wall. And Grandpa Howard was a bigamist who had disappeared for ten years and who, when he wasn't at work, sat half asleep in the Queen Anne armchair in a dark corner of his living room. Once an hour he came out of his musings to say: "Aw, shit!" He would goose his daughters whenever they came within reach of his armchair so hard that they sometimes cried.

After their fourth cup of coffee and many cigarettes later, my aunts would proceed to the bathroom to put on their faces. They welcomed an audience during their makeup rituals. So Sally and I squeezed into the cramped, poorly ventilated bathroom, full of cigarette smoke, with its claw-footed tub and mildewed blue-and-pink tile. We would trade places standing on the toilet to observe these joyful exhibitionists. It took them more than an hour to make themselves presentable. Sally and I took breaks to eat peanut-butter-and-jelly sandwiches on Wonder bread, the only food in the house.

Aunt Lilly and Aunt Daisy began by eyeing each other in the small mirror. "Oh, God, are you ever an ugly schmuck!" "Well, you're uglier!" Though at the time, they were thirty-six and thirty-seven respectively, they appeared a lot older to me, perhaps because they were so tough and raw. Their caustic, crude talk always startled me. In the upscale suburb where I was from, we were taught to act like ladies. Yet, even during some of their most heated arguments, a strange, twisted sense of humor came through that was unique to Dad's side of the family. I couldn't understand it, but I appreciated it somehow.

"She's too obnoxious to ever die," is how Sally often described Aunt Daisy. But Sally wasn't afraid to talk back to her mom, which I admired, especially since I was afraid to talk back to mine. And sometimes Sally amazed me when she defended her shrewish mom. "She always does what she wants in life, and how many people can you say do that?" True, I thought, uncomforted. What if Aunt Daisy or Aunt Lilly had been my mother? I contemplated with horror. Because they were my aunts, that possibility was more than real.

Although Lilly and Daisy looked like sisters, they parlayed themselves into identical twins with almost identical makeup, clothes, wigs,

Janice J. Heiss

expressions, and mannerisms. They even lived parallel lives: first and foremost, shopping and eating out day in and day out. And they had the same clique of friends—bowling with the Gutter Gals, Temple Shalom's sisterhood team; playing bingo, mah-jongg, canasta, and pinochle; chain-smoking; and gossiping on the phone for hours.

Still, Aunt Daisy and Aunt Lilly competed in every conceivable way: from their husbands, Benny and Harry; their incomes; the year, make, and size of their cars; and who caused, ended, and won all their fights. They each had two children, first a boy and then a girl. They each had one good child, the boy, and a bad, disappointing child, the girl.

"Starting from scratch," as they called it, they applied beige makeup base from their faces to their necklines. They looked ghastly, like murderers hovering over a bed wearing tight, transparent, flesh-colored stockings that squished their features. They plucked their natural eyebrows and penciled in glistening, perfect half circles, high above where their original eyebrows used to be. With dark, dried-blood-red lipstick pencil, they outlined brand-new big lips. When I told Aunt Daisy that I could see the outline of her thin, natural lips, she shooed me away, saying: "Just stand back a ways, kid." They always matched their lipstick color to their outfit, choosing from a shelf full of lipsticks with names like Really Red, Pink Bouton, or Orange Sportif. My aunts chose Coral Reef that day to apply inside their dark lip outlines.

Like knifeless plastic surgeons, they fashioned cheekbones from face powder and cream rouge, creating two rash-colored "ski slopes." Eyes came next. They layered colored eye shadow like a graduated color chart from their lashes to eyebrows. With eyeliner, they penciled in across their eyelids shiny, thick black uneven lines, that looked like tire skid marks by the end of the day. Extra-long, fake eyelashes formed awnings over their eyes. No matter what glue they used, their eyelashes fell off. On holidays my aunts used so much eye makeup, I didn't know how they could open and close their eyes. Beauty marks were the final touch, drawn to enhance facial moles with black and brown makeup pencils. I automatically shrank from my aunts when they greeted me with their customary kiss because their beauty marks left smudges.

My aunts swore their husbands had never seen them without makeup. Aunt Daisy said no one but Sally, me, and the surgeon who operated on her had ever seen her without her face on. "No one sees or hears you without your makeup on," was one of my aunts' credos. Aunt Lilly even touched up her makeup before having dental X rays.

Aunt Daisy and Aunt Lilly were nearly bald, the greatest tragedy to befall them. Still, they fought constantly over who was the natural red-head. Their fine mousy-brown, cotton-candy-textured hair looked as though it had been pulled out in clumps. Since they wore their wigs to bed, I saw their bald heads only once, through the bathroom-door key-hole, as they exchanged wigs one Thanksgiving. They wore identical synthetic brassy, orange wigs that cost $9.99 and came in one style only—a full-bodied bubble, selected from the faded mannequin heads in the crowded window of Skokie's main Woolworth's.

By the time their makeup was settled, as they called it, and after several more cups of coffee and a pack of cigarettes each, my aunts were finally ready to go out for lunch, a highlight of their day. Because my aunts often expressed their hostility toward each other in public, many family members refused to dine out with them to avoid the humiliation.

"So, where should we eat today?" Pyrotechnics followed until one of my aunts gave in, and Sally and I found ourselves in the spacious back-seat of Aunt Lilly's old red-and-white Edsel on our way to the Double-T Wagon Restaurant, an inexpensive, bustling, midwestern ranch-style restaurant better known for its twenty-four-hour service than for its food.

"I can't eat this. I taste sugar in it," Aunt Lilly said, pushing her alphabet vegetable soup away, always sure she was on the verge of a diabetes diagnosis.

"Oh, don't give me that shit. There's absolutely nothing wrong with your sugar, Miss Ishy," replied Aunt Daisy. "You're off your rocker, sis."

"Mom, please keep it down," Sally tried to interject.

"And shut up, kid," Aunt Daisy said to Sally. "You're homely and you have a fresh mouth. Keep it up and no man will ever marry you." Sally impressed me every time she tried to stand up to her big bad witch of a mother. But sometimes mother and daughter would gang up on Aunt Lilly and together laugh that ear-shattering, evil Wicked-Witch-of-the-West laugh that made me want to duck for cover. Was my cousin more like her mom than I thought?

"You're awfully quiet," observed Aunt Lilly when she saw my wide-

Janice J. Heiss

eyed gaze. Sally kicked me under the table and gave me an encouraging look.

"No, no, fine. Just eating," I said. Aunt Lilly could be nice when she wanted to. Maybe she didn't want me to go home and report them to my mom and dad.

Sally and I gobbled down our Sloppy Joes and started rolling our eyes and making faces at each other out of boredom and disgust with Lilly and Daisy. We choked on the smoke as my aunts dawdled and picked at their food, chain-smoking throughout the meal. The ashtray overflowed onto the table, so my aunts began putting out their butts in their plates. Aunt Lilly drew a nauseating butt-face in her egg yolk.

"What a horrible waitress!" said Aunt Lilly, the cheaper sister. Her opinion of the service invariably declined through the meal, hitting bottom right before tip time. "Just look at that ashtray. She didn't even bother, sis."

"Yes, she hardly deserves a tip," Aunt Daisy agreed.

"Well, we gotta give her something, I guess. After all, we come here a lot."

Aunt Daisy and Aunt Lilly dug inside their matching black patent-leather purses for small change as Sally and I, sensing a fight, slid down in the red vinyl booth.

"How about fifty cents total, generous for this crap," Aunt Daisy proposed. "What do you think, little sis?"

"Do I look like I'm made of money?" responded Aunt Lilly. "My soup was cold and had sugar in it. The dumb ass could have killed me and could care less."

"How do you know? You hardly touched it, you ding-dong hypochondriac!" replied Aunt Daisy, mocking Aunt Lilly by scrunching her face and sticking out her tongue.

"Y'know, you act just like Dad," said Lilly. This below-the-belt comment always stung.

After endless back and forth, they decided on a 6 percent tip, using the paper place mat to do the math. Aunt Lilly said, "Let me see. I don't seem to have the right change for my part of the tip. Can you spare a nickel?"

"Y'know, everyone calls you a little piker behind your back, sis," said Aunt Daisy, her voice becoming shrill.

"Well, okay, Miss Smarty-Pants, be that way and I'll just tip five cents less," Aunt Lilly said.

Here it comes, I thought, slouching down farther in my seat. Sally gave me a knowing look. As their conflict escalated, everyone in the restaurant turned and gawked at us.

"Oh, shut up, you snotty puss! No wonder Mom always—"

"No, you shut up, you crybaby!"

"Go to hell."

When the wife of the Double-T Wagon's Greek owner approached our table, I contemplated mutiny. But I was too afraid. I felt as though someone had pushed me on stage under a blinding spotlight, and I had forgotten all my lines. I didn't hear anything that the owner's wife said.

Aunt Daisy stared straight ahead. She dropped her voice ten octaves, easy for a three-pack-a-day smoker, and growled in a deep, menacing voice, "Are you telling me to leave your restaurant, miss, because I don't really think you want to do that." I stole a glance to see if she had begun to foam at the mouth. Before the owner's wife could respond, Aunt Daisy said with a bit of levity, "It's a free country, isn't it? And besides, we're kissing cousins." She grabbed Aunt Lilly's hand across the table, gripping it so tightly it left a red imprint on Aunt Lilly's arm. Aunt Lilly winced but went along with her sister.

Sally, looking tormented, kicked me under the table. "Mom, will you please, please stop!" she yelled.

"Honey, take it easy," Aunt Daisy said sarcastically.

"After all, it wouldn't be good for business for you to cause a real scene in your restaurant, would it?" sneered Aunt Daisy, never looking up at the proprietress.

Everything went to fast-forward. As the owner's wife backed off sheepishly from the table, and my aunts returned to their argument, Sally disappeared and reappeared in seconds with two pies from the pie case. She handed an apple pie to me while throwing a banana cream pie in her mother's face! Bananas and cream dripped off her wig and face. I heard a scream of joy and then one of horror from somewhere, and I felt dizzy and disoriented.

Janice J. Heiss

"Do it!" I heard Sally yell through the bedlam and food mist, and the next thing I knew I pied Aunt Lilly. Food, crust, apples, custard all over everything! Table, chairs, down my blouse, on Lilly's glasses. My aunts shrieked in fury and delight, and was that a smile on Aunt Daisy's face as she and Lilly started flinging food all over the place?

"You little brats," someone screamed, as I felt some syrupy liquid on my back and something hard hit against the back of my leg as I stumbled on a wet spot on my way out the door after the restaurant-wide food fight started.

We ran for blocks and blocks, too confused to understand but knowing something big had changed.

Aunt Daisy recently died at age eighty-two, after smoking three packs of unfiltered Camels a day until she had to go on oxygen. Sally told me that her mother had mellowed by her late seventies. On her deathbed, Aunt Daisy let down her guard as she and Sally discussed how she used to frighten people. My aunt told Sally that in her day, she had to be tough to get respect. "You all have more options now," she said. "Maybe if I had been born in your generation, I would have been a women's libber," she said, half joking. "Sneak me a cigarette, will you, hon, while the nurse is gone?"

New York Aunties

Subtle Choices

RAQUELLE AZRAN

Growing old offers a choice. You can fade away into an inoffensive shadow, or you can become larger than life. My aunt Enid chose the latter option.

Enid was actually my mother's first cousin. Her parents died when she was young, and she was raised by my grandparents, first in London and then in New York. She became a devoted older sister to my mother, as outspoken and fearless as my mother was proper and restrained.

My aunt Enid was never known for her subtlety. We avoided her as children, fearing her barbed tongue. As she stalked around in stiletto heels with a bleached-blonde chignon and a scarlet smear of lipstick on her lips, Enid was an enigma in our world of motherly aunties. There was nothing soft or cuddly about her.

Enid drove her aging silver Cadillac badly but with bravado, careening from lane to lane, daring other drivers—"Come kiss my fender, yahoo!"—to cramp her style. At the weekly Thursday evening bridge game with my parents, Enid flashed her cards with long scarlet fingernails. My father glared as she punctured his concentration with barks of laughter. Perched on the stairs to our bedroom, my brother and I strained to catch Enid's outrageous comments and delighted in repeating them to each other before going to bed: "You underbidding zucchini," "Give your mind a good mothball," or "Cut the deck, Daddy-O."

If Enid was too large for our world, her husband was small and mean. Harry was a sandy-colored, sparse-haired man of indistinct height and weight. The only remarkable thing about him was his nasty laugh. He called his statuesque wife "fatso," and we children steered clear of him like poison, not wanting to risk hearing his pet names for us. His meanness was corrosive, unrelenting, as if he felt he had nothing more to lose.

Caught up in the selfish excitement of childhood, we never even realized that Enid was childless. Only when her criticism of our behavior and appearance exposed Enid's ignorance of adolescent peer pressure (an utter ignorance of adolescent norms) did we wake up to the fact that no one had ever called Enid "Mom."

"You were much prettier without all that hair in your face and makeup smeared on your eyes," she once chided me when I was thirteen. "You would walk more gracefully without those ridiculous platform shoes."

"How absurd to start shaving when all you have is a bit of fuzz on your lip," she told my fourteen-year-old brother.

"I'm not listening to her anymore," my brother said disgustedly. "She doesn't have a clue about kids. Just keep her away from me."

Somewhere around the age of fifty, Enid took up designing jewelry. You have to understand, no one in our family is artsy: no fashion designers, no interior decorators, not even a hair stylist. Then Enid began to wear her creations, bulky packages of silver and turquoise, on her fingers, on her earlobes, and hanging between her stiffly uplifted breasts. Her new friends, potters and weavers, shaped clay and spun wool in secluded cottages. To be near them, she bought a house in Woodstock, New York, with a burbling brook in the backyard and possums bedding down in the chimney. Then one night, small, mean Harry died unexpectedly in his sleep. And it was about that time when Enid chose how to grow old. She sold the house in Woodstock and moved back to the hustle of the city.

"I bet I can attract more men at a singles bar than you can," she challenged me. And she did. Too brash to be ignored and still unmotherly, Enid attracted shy young men by the armload. They saw, under her bluster, the neediness that we had missed.

The superintendent in her New York City apartment building was the first to notice. "Excuse me, Mrs. Blocker," he mumbled, staring fixedly at the tip of his boot. "The neighbors are complaining about a lot of strange men showing up at your apartment."

Enid boomed her infamous laugh, the one that set the dogs howling and everyone's teeth on edge. "You're absolutely right, honey. Just tell the neighbors to speak to me directly."

Only after my thirtieth birthday did Enid and I become friends. She criticized my makeup, roughly informed me that only underwire bras would support a drooping bosom, and grandly bestowed upon me her cast-off high heels. We companionably smoked long brown cigarettes in jade holders, sitting in her overheated apartment on brocade armchairs grown shabby. I became Enid's audience and was rewarded with vivid tales of family skeletons.

"Look at the engagement photograph of your mother. Now look at her wedding photograph. Find the difference," Enid commanded. I looked at both photos. They were definitely both my mom.

"Look again, carefully," she insisted. I stared. The hair? The makeup? The nose? The nose! Mom's nose was different. The bulbous engagement nose had metamorphosed into a sleek wedding nose. "Mom had a nose job," I said, amazed at my discovery.

"Your father demanded she get it done. He also insisted she lose weight before the wedding. I remember your mother, dizzy from hunger, but starving herself to please your father."

Fiercely protective, I debated Enid's merits with assorted family members as they tried to evade her calls and avoid her visits. "She's witty. She has a great sense of humor. Just give her a chance," I begged my brother. "She has a great sense of style, she can give you some ideas for redecorating the house," I told my sister-in-law. "Dad, if you invite Enid for Saturday lunch, I'll come, too," I bargained craftily. Anything was better than having Enid steadily drink her way through solitary weekends.

As the years passed, Enid's hair grew brassier, her loud voice even more strident. Accompanying Enid to the theater or a museum meant enduring annoyed looks and shushes from everyone in the vicinity of her voice. Never overly generous, she became addicted to ninety-nine-cent bargains—a key holder, hairpins, cheap notepaper, which she would gift wrap and hand out at holiday gatherings. With fewer and fewer friends to talk to, she became a nuisance on the telephone, calling

Raquelle Azran

97

me at strange hours of the night and prattling for hours. Finally she announced that we all bored her to death and that she was going off to Alaska.

"Alaska, Enid? What are you going to do in Alaska?"

"I'll have a ball there," she said. "Lots of strong men in Alaska. Besides, I've never been there."

"Come on, Enid. Who's going to look after you, so far away?"

"The same people who aren't looking after me here. Do you really think I'm blind to how they look at me, what they say about me? In Alaska, the Eskimos treat old people with respect. When it's all over, the old folks walk off in the snow and freeze to death with dignity. And by God, I'll die with dignity, too."

I get an occasional postcard from Alaska, with scrawled lines of pure energy singing tales of life. It seems the issue of dying has receded into the future. I picture Enid surrounded by adoring weather-beaten fishermen, her raucous voice chastened by ice floes. She brings tenderness and excitement into their lives.

A New York Smile

MARLO BROOKS

As an only child of divorced working parents, I was used to being bounced around among family or friends for hours, and sometimes days, at a time. Though visits from my long-distant father were infrequent, I had somehow grown accustomed to his big hugs, flashy smile, and deep laughter. People would often comment that I have the mirror image of that toothy grin. These affirmations gave me a keen sense of knowing that I belonged to him. But by the time I was five years old, I still hadn't met any of his ten siblings or his dozens of nieces and nephews. His East Coast family was a mystery to me. But on one fateful afternoon I was transported from the sunny comforts of California to the bleak, cold reality of a wintry New York City. I was not delivered into the familiar animated hands of my father, but into the arms of a stranger, his sister, my aunt Serena.

I was a thin brown-skinned girl with long bangs and knobby knees. As the plane's interior lights flickered on, I kneeled desperately on the cabin floor, praying to become invisible. I knew my aunt was waiting for me. She and her husband, Uncle James, had agreed to raise me in their Spanish Harlem apartment along with her two children. Passengers pulled coats, luggage, and beautifully wrapped packages from various compartments of the plane as I waited for them to disembark so I could go back to San Diego. I assumed that airplanes worked like buses and that in a matter of minutes we would be on our way back to palm trees and sandy beaches. A gentle tug at my collar ended my attempted getaway.

I was quickly ushered off and escorted into a throng of bustling New York faces. I heard excitement as a small group made its way toward my trembling body. I don't know if I was more afraid of the smiling faces

Marlo Brooks

rushing toward me or that the only door to take me back home had been sealed with a thud.

Modestly dressed in bulky clothing and a very large pocketbook, Aunt Serena called out in a heavy New York accent, "Mawlo!" She grabbed me in a giant hug and planted kisses all over my crying face. "Baby, you had me worried. I saw everyone else come off that plane, but I didn't see my Mawlo."

I looked at her, my cousins, and my pretty-boy uncle, but I couldn't find any traces of home. On my mother's side of the family were sand-colored women with light eyes and European features. My father was the color of dark coal, and Serena was the color of oak with dark weathered limbs and hands, much closer to handsome than pretty.

"Doesn't she look like her fawtha," Aunt Serena called out to her daughter Barbara. "And look at those dimples." Barbara rolled her eyes and shrugged her shoulders behind Aunt Serena's back. Though we were six years apart, I was fierce competition, and unknowingly became an unlikely threat to my new roommate.

"Yeah, if that ain't Green," my uncle added, calling my father by his and my last name. He gave me a big hug and kissed me, too. "You gonna be my baby girl," he added. Again Barbara rolled her eyes.

"These your cousins Irvin and Bawbwa," Aunt Serena introduced with great pride. Irvin was three years older and seemed happy to meet me, but Barbara's rolling eyes spoke volumes. "Now, let's get your suitcase and take you home."

Uncle James popped Donny Hathaway's "This Christmas" into the eight-track and steered his sleek 1971 Buick Riviera through the cold streets of New York. Aunt Serena held me close as she began to tell me all the things I was going to do and see. She was trying to spark a conversation, but I had nothing to say.

"I told Santa you were coming, and he's going to bring all your presents to our house." I closed my eyes and frowned. I didn't want Santa Claus; I wanted my mother.

"You like books? I got lots of books." Aunt Serena offered.

"Those are my books," Barbara called from the backseat. Her comment was addressed with a quick glance from Uncle James.

Aunt Serena went on and on about the new life I was going to have with them in New York. The more she talked, the sadder I became. In all of her plans, I never heard when my father would be coming or when I would see my mom again. Somewhere inside I was beginning to despise this Aunt Serena. The car finally came to a stop; I blinked twice. The picture before me bloomed of hopelessness.

I had never seen a housing project before. It was incredibly intimidating. Each building was exactly the same, though the graffiti gave each its personal flavor. A burnt-car smell hovered around Aunt Serena's building. I would have been satisfied if we had never left Donny and the Buick, for the world outside looked frightening. With a careful prod, Aunt Serena guided me toward the elevator while Uncle James found a place to park.

"This is it, your new home!" Aunt Serena pushed the door open to a cramped but cheery apartment. A large Christmas tree glowed in the corner near a window. There were gifts piled underneath and bowls of fruits and nuts everywhere. Barbara shoved past me and disappeared down a narrow hall. Irvin plopped on a plastic-covered couch and threw his leg over the arm. Aunt Serena began pulling off her coat and hat and assisted me with mine.

She took me on a tour that ended with the bed I would be sharing with my cousin Barbara. She finally asked if I had any questions. I was surprised to hear myself say, "Yes."

"When will my daddy come get me?" I knew he wasn't coming.

"He's going to visit you as soon as he can. He has that good job that keeps him traveling, but he's going to call you tonight." She looked as if she was telling the truth, but I didn't want to believe her. I wanted to believe that she was lying and that my mom would come rescue me after she realized that Aunt Serena planned to keep me.

"What about my mommy?"

"Mawlo, your mommy is going to go to school, and when she's ready, she'll send for you so you can visit."

"When will I get to live with her?"

"Your fawtha will be able to answer all these questions when he calls tonight." I knew I was making her uncomfortable.

Marlo Brooks

"But why do I have to live here? With you?"

"You don't want to live with me?" She looked surprised and a little hurt.

"No."

"Why not?" I didn't expect a question. I didn't know what to say. So I blurted, "Because you don't know how to do my hair."

"What do you mean, I don't know how to do your hair. I can make your hair look pretty. Real pretty. I promise."

"Nu-uh." Tears began to fall.

"Yes I can."

"No, you can't!" I screamed and then cried into my small hands. Aunt Serena pulled me close, which made me cry harder. I could smell her. It was a light flowery smell that reminded me that she wasn't my mother. My mother didn't wear perfumes or fragrant lotions. She always smelled like oatmeal soap and her daily tray of vitamins.

"Go ahead and let it all out, baby. You just go on ahead and cry," Aunt Serena stroked my back with one hand and pulled off the rubber bands that held my two loose ponytails with the other.

"What happened to her?" Barbara came rushing in with a smile.

"She's all right. Go get the stuff I use to do your hair and set it up."

"For what?"

"Do as I say, now!"

Barbara's eyes rolled.

Uncle James came in holding my small red suitcase and looking bewildered. "What's going on with the baby girl?"

"She's going to be all right. She's missing her mom right now."

I almost lost my breath. I was shocked that she knew.

"Can I make you feel better?" She held my chin up. "I think I know how."

We walked into a small yellow- and brown-stained kitchen. There were freshly baked cookies on a plate on the center of the stove. Barbara had pulled out a comb and brush, towel, straightening comb, jar of pressing oil, and a giant canister filled with barrettes in a magnificent bouquet of vibrant colors. Aunt Serena sat me on a stool by the stove and gave me the canister to hold. There were so many different shades and shapes that it was almost overwhelming. My mother only used rubber bands and occasionally a ribbon.

Aunt Serena placed the towel around my shoulders, turned on a burner, and stuck the iron straightening comb into the flame. Someone turned on music, and Aunt Serena began to sing along. She handed me a cookie and asked me to choose the barrettes I wanted to wear in my hair.

I really didn't want to get my hair straightened. But Aunt Serena didn't look as if she was going to give me an option. As soon as the comb sliced through a section of my hair, it bowed down in one mighty swoon and rested on my back.

I was nervous. I hoped she wouldn't accidentally burn me or make me look funny. I have a high forehead and wore bangs to keep my face balanced. I sat there at her mercy and prayed she didn't take away my bangs.

"You are going to look like a movie star, Mawlo," she promised. Each time she combed through another section, Aunt Serena was careful not to let the heat touch me. The whole time she complimented my hair, my smile, even my sherbet-pink-colored fingernails. Aunt Serena was determined to win the battle I had declared

I was reaching for my fifth chocolate-chip cookie when she handed me a mirror. My hair had never been pressed so quickly before. To my delight, I saw a brilliant rainbow of barrettes sitting above a neat row of bangs. The unexpected image produced my first New York smile.

"You like it?" Aunt Serena asked with her hands on her full hips. Everyone had gathered around, nodding approval. Even Barbara's eyes didn't roll away at the sight of my dazzling bejeweled crown.

"Yes, I like it!" I nodded eagerly. I really thought I looked like a movie star. "You're gonna do my hair like this *all* the time?" I asked with a mouth full of cookie.

"Yes, baby. Every day."

"For real?"

"I promise."

"You promise promise?"

"Yes, baby, I promise promise." I smiled at the pretty girl in the mirror.

In my thirty-four years Aunt Serena would be the only person in my life who never broke a promise.

Marlo Brooks

_____

Aunt Nellie's Trousseau

MARY MARINO McCARTHY

The sheets are white, their borders a wonder of single, double, and triple crochet stitches.

In the early 1900s, when she and the New York subway were young, my great-aunt Nellie took her handwork with her each day on the ride to work in the garment district. I can picture her, her crochet hook flying and her body swaying with the rhythm of the train.

As a child, I labored under her intense eyes to maneuver yarn with my large, beginner's hook. Aunt Nellie would tell me how total strangers admired her work and how she could crochet with her eyes closed. It was easy for me to conjure an image of her crocheting away on the subway until she neared her stop and opened her eyes to regally acknowledge admiring gazes before gathering up her work and sweeping out through the doors.

Carmela Marino, known as Nellie, was a tall woman, handsome and erect, with a commanding presence. My aunt didn't walk, she marched. Her dark brown eyes flashed; she brooked no challenges from my sisters or me. Her broad shoulders tapered to slim legs, and her gray hair was rinsed to silver. She had snapping brown eyes, a strict personality, and a loving heart. I now have the sheets with the lace crochet borders that she crafted—and never used—for her trousseau almost a century ago.

When she was a girl, Aunt Nellie made and collected items for her wedding trousseau, her "hope chest." But she never married; a series of childhood illnesses and a lifelong bleeding disorder contributed to her single life. On rare occasion, she talked wistfully about a special girlhood flirtation, which in the strict times of her youth took place through secret glances and small encounters, usually at church.

When I was young, her hands were gnarled and arthritic, but they still could make a crochet hook fly. Her fine crochet work was a source of special pride. She had learned it from her mother, and in turn taught my mother, then my sisters and me. She told me that as a girl she had been punished for mistakes, forced to kneel on bags of dried chickpeas until the stitches were completed properly. By comparison, Aunt Nellie was a gentle teacher, who merely ripped out yards of our careful stitches to correct an error so we could begin again.

Her parents, my great-grandparents, emigrated from Italy and made a life in America with simple labors. Her father was a sanitation worker, who took seriously his responsibility to sweep the city streets clean. Her mama had an entrepreneurial spirit and earned extra money doing everything from piecework at home to turning their living room into a small café to selling furniture and jewelry on consignment to future newlyweds. Aunt Nellie was active in all her mama's enterprises.

Because Nellie had seven brothers and sisters and needed to help her family, she began taking the subway at age sixteen, traveling from 111th Street to the Garment District on West Thirty-fourth Street. During her daily trip, she crocheted elaborate table scarves, three-dimensional squares for bedspreads, and lace borders on handkerchiefs. In the factory, she applied intricate hand beading to sparkling flapper dresses and debutante gowns. Later in life, she made silk flowers and was promoted to supervisor. The jewel-toned flowers she made still brighten the houses in our family. At home she knit and crocheted, and took pride in it all.

For her trousseau linens, Aunt Nellie had crocheted the wide, lacy borders in long strips and then sewed them onto oversized sheeting yardage. To my surprise, I found black lettering stamped SECONDS onto some corners. The challenge of her times in a single word.

While she seemed content with her single life, Aunt Nellie never used her beautiful, handmade trousseau linens. For years they rested, neatly folded in a box in my mother's attic. I had been married for several years when my mother asked if I would like them. I put them on my bed for the first time with trepidation. I sank into the wooden chair in my bedroom and simply gazed at them. They gleamed. White sheets

*Mary Marino
McCarthy*

105

and pillowcases with intricate six-inch, hand-crocheted borders. They were nearly too beautiful to use. I have treasured the linens now for over a quarter century, and their beauty has never faded.

The fiber of the old cotton is the most comfortable fabric I have known, especially in summer when the sheets are blessedly cool on hot nights. They were a comfort to my mind and body during chemotherapy treatment several years ago, when powerful drugs brought on terrible night sweats. Aunt Nellie's spirit was surely at work to sooth and comfort me as I slept.

Her robust spirit was evident when I came down with a childhood illness during a holiday visit to Aunt Nellie. By then, my father's job had transferred us to Albany in upstate New York, and Aunt Nellie lived in Brooklyn, working as a supervisor in an artificial flower factory. It was Easter Sunday, and I was just sick enough and just old enough to stay behind while everyone went to church around the corner. But Aunt Nellie must have been unsure about leaving me alone. After church, she marched into her apartment, face stern with worry, arm already outstretched to feel my forehead for signs of lingering fever. I can still recall the sight of her striding through the door and my spontaneous realization: She loves me—a lot!

Aunt Nellie's nurturing streak was as powerful as the garlic she tied in a handkerchief around her neck when she felt a cold approaching. She doted on her great-nieces as she had doted on my mother when Mom was a girl. My mother's voice still sparkles when she speaks of her regular excursions with Aunt Nellie to the silent movies, and then early talking movies, which were an inexpensive escape during the Depression. My aunt spent vacations and part of the summer with us, and she helped my mother, who worked full-time. She had a forceful personality, but there was never any doubt of her love.

My aunt loved to do things with style. Her "hello" rose three octaves on the second syllable when she answered the phone. She never met any caller at the door informally. In the flash of an eye, Aunt Nellie would put down the potato she was peeling, whip off her apron, administer a healthy dollop of face powder, and complete her transformation with an application of her favorite deep red Hazel Bishop lipstick.

On family picnics, Aunt Nellie whipped up complete meals on a portable Coleman stove. She had taught my mother her secrets for homemade macaroni, and now she passed those lessons on to my sisters and me. Other cooks might allow their ravioli to form amorphous shapes, but Aunt Nellie had high standards: nothing but perfect circles would do. Our small hands busily pressed the coffeepot lid into the dough after her rolling pin had made its last swipe. Each circle then received a dollop of filling and was folded into a half moon, ready to be finished off. We sealed her ravioli by neat presses with the tines of a fork, completing each one with a flourish and a soft jab in the center to make air holes for cooking. The results were perfection. And if you weren't sure, Aunt Nellie told you so.

My aunt was a proud woman, proud of her family, her Italian heritage, and her talents. She taught us to use our talents and to take pride in whatever task we undertook—from our studies to sweeping the floor to crafting things. She taught us that nurturing a family was an important role. And she taught us to value beauty and to see it every day, whether in a well-ironed shirt seam, a garden, or the skilled work of an artisan.

She appreciated fine things, jewelry and furniture, and later in life, she indulged as her finances allowed. My mother tells me that pawnshops were sometimes a necessary part of life, when jewelry was treasured but was also an investment that could help a family through financial ebbs and flows. Aunt Nellie was determined that her jewelry be passed on, giving each sister a vintage piece. One birthday, she gave me her aquamarine ring, my birthstone.

On special occasions my aunt gave us keepsakes. I still remember choosing with sweet deliberation a bracelet of gold swirls and hearts for my sixteenth birthday. Now, my daughter wears those delicate gold swirls and hearts.

Aunt Nellie even showed us how to grow old with spunk. As a young teen, I once visited her on my own, and she marched me around the highlights of Manhattan, complaining about her bunions as I hurried to keep up with her. She laughed and, sighing dramatically, suggested that I should try not to grow old. And now that arthritis has touched my limbs, I understand.

Mary Marino
McCarthy

107

When I was a young wife, and the sheets were new to me, I washed them with little concern for wear and tear. After all, I told myself, Aunt Nellie would have boiled them on washday, then put them through a wringer. I baby the sheets now, using them only when some special need calls. I use the shortest, mildest wash cycle, sparing them the clothes dryer that I once used so recklessly. Instead, it is a pleasure to hang them outside to dry. My grown son, Michael, home one weekend, carried the laundry basket out for me. Together, we folded the sheets lengthwise to keep them from dragging on the grass, and then, our hands mingling and reaching to the sky, we hung them on the line. As we stood in the sun, the cotton dancing around us on a breeze, I felt the flow and strength of four generations. Later that day, I carefully folded Aunt Nellie's sheets and put them away, knowing there would be a time when they would soothe me again.

Aunt Nellie's Special Company Ravioli

DOUGH
1 pound flour
1 egg
1 cup water
1 tsp salt
Drop of oil

Place flour in bowl or on a large wood cutting board. Form a hollow or well in the dough and add other ingredients. Mix until a workable dough.

FILLING
2 pounds ricotta cheese to 1 egg
¼ cup grated cheese
Pepper to taste

Roll dough to thickness similar to pie crust. Use a circular cookie cutter to make round circles of dough for each ravioli. Drop filling onto dough. Fold into semicircle and seal, pressing around the open edges with the flat tines of a fork. Put air holes in top with one gentle jab with the fork.

Boil in a large saucepan for about 6 to 8 minutes or until dough is tender.

Mary Marino
McCarthy

The Power of the Triangle

M. CECILE FORTE

"All right now, come give Aunt Pauline some sugar!"

That was her greeting whenever she gathered each of her nieces into her arms and smothered us with hugs against her ample, sweet-smelling bosom. Thinking about her now, I can still smell the Arpège that perfumed her space. Aunt Pauline was our only relative who wore real French perfume, recommending that we girls adopt a "signature fragrance." Lord, we loved to hear Aunt Pauline talk. She worked at being refined; she believed life was about becoming, so the fact that she worked in a factory was only what she did, not who she was. Coming from a poor family, I benefited from her philosophy. I never felt bogged down by my beginnings, only lifted up by my possibilities. Even now, whatever I achieve brings me pleasure because I have accomplished a higher and better purpose, not just overcome obstacles. I realize now that Aunt Pauline instilled that attitude in me at an early age.

If you didn't really know her, you might think Aunt Pauline was "putting on airs," trying to be more than she was, and she would agree with you. "I believe in looking up," she'd say. "Look down and you might find a safety pin, a pen, or a five-dollar bill on the sidewalk if you're lucky. But just look up, and the sun, moon, and stars are yours."

"I'll take the five-dollar bill and give you the heavens, Pauline," was Uncle Fred's reply. Always loving, he sometimes teased her but was never critical of his Pauline. Smiling a that's-why-I-love-you smile for the man she married when she was seventeen, she felt content although she was well aware that her sisters believed she was a dreamer who lived beyond her means and had no regard for money.

"That's my sister, and I love her, but . . ." my mother always said. She never completed the rest of that sentence. Her loyalty was stronger than her need to criticize. Besides, Mama and Daddy dedicated their lives to making a better life for us kids, and that took every penny they earned. Mama made and sold homemade candy and even booked numbers in the summertime to make ends meet. Daddy was a shipping clerk at a warehouse during the week and washed cars on the weekend. Poverty taught them how to survive, and they were experts at it. Aunt Pauline's "fake it till you make it" philosophy was understandably incomprehensible to my parents, Myrt and Bill.

Make no mistake, Aunt Pauline's human failings were part of my life's equation as well. Looking back, I realize she genuinely loved Uncle Fred despite her indiscretions. She kept various boyfriends on the side as a kind of testament to her need to compete with her sisters, whom she always felt were prettier, more fertile—and therefore, to her mind, better than she was. She couldn't change her looks, she couldn't make babies, but she could attract men. It was her pastime, her heartrending claim to fame. Now I can see her choices as both wise and reckless. But as a child I accepted that she needed more than most to be happy. And it was just that kind of thinking that made Aunt Pauline our very own Auntie Mame.

She lived in Harlem where her Sugar Hill address provided a panoramic view of the city below and the river beyond. Uncle Fred worked at the post office, a plum job in the days when few black men were given more opportunity. But his side jobs (Uncle Fred could fix anything) allowed Aunt Pauline to live her life in style. Visiting Aunt Pauline and Uncle Fred was nothing short of adventurous. Back then Sundays were all about church and family dinners. Some kids got to go to the movies after the meal. No such luck in our family, there was no shortchanging the Creator. We kept the Sabbath "wholly." So when it was our turn to visit Aunt Pauline, we were excited. Three prepubescent, knobby-kneed, awkward, skinny girls dressed hurriedly, went to mass at Our Lady of Victory, walked back home and waited for Mama and Daddy to come down and meet us in the vestibule of our Brooklyn apartment house.

Daddy left the car wash with just enough time to dress for dinner. When not at work, Daddy always wore a tie. There was none of the usual whining, complaining, and arguing. We were on our way to Aunt Pauline's.

Heading into Manhattan from Queens, we picked up Grandpa in Ozone Park, crossed the Triborough Bridge, and waited for the New York skyline to appear. On 125th Street, folks strolled the boulevard, ladies in hats and gloves, men in suits, children in Sunday shoes, Bibles in their hands, and I imagined the family dinners they would have. It was April, and Daddy rolled down the car windows. I sat in the back as always and let the wind force my bangs off my forehead and hold them straight up in the air. My green ribbons were intact, braided into my pigtails; Mama would take care of my bangs before we got to Aunt Pauline's apartment. Deidre and Renee wore yellow dresses that were just alike because they were twins. Yellow ribbons completed the ensemble.

We entered Aunt Pauline's Convent Avenue building by the side entrance, closest to where Daddy parked. The smell of dinners cooking throughout the building made me suddenly hungry. The elevator rose quickly to the ninth floor. Uncle Fred answered the door and behind him were family members already assembled for the feast. Aunt Pauline was a terrific cook who was proud of her round body and, like the rest of her sisters, made no effort to diet because they had no need to be slim. Poor people are happy when they have food to eat and bodies to prove it.

"You all come on in here. Glad to see you all."

We embraced our family; the kids hit the chips and dip immediately. Uncle Fred handed out sodas: black cherry, grape, orange, and ginger ale. Mama and Grandmama warned us about drinking too much too fast. And then Aunt Pauline appeared.

"All right now, give Aunt Pauline some sugar!"

She had freckles under her eyes, and her hair was a light reddish brown. Aunt Pauline's skin was the color of butterscotch, and she had hazel eyes. She was pleasant-looking because of the laughter in her life, and she genuinely enjoyed what she had. Uncle Fred thought she was absolutely beautiful. She used to say teasingly that was because he was getting old and didn't see well. But she loved and thrived on his praise. He was her husband, her supporter, her confidant, a substitute for the child she never had, and he was determined to make her happy. Whatever losses, turmoil, disappointments, or trouble that came Pauline's way were his to bear. In his white shirt, tie, and dark trousers soaking wet, he weighed less than 150 pounds. But he could slay dragons with the best of them. She wore a soft green floor-length caftan with black embroidery. I thought she looked beautiful, too.

Aunt Pauline gave us many gifts. Gifts she might have given a child of her own. The greatest of all charmed our souls: she treated us like adults. As early as age five or six, in addition to the usual "How's school?" "What's your favorite color?" "How will you spend your summer?" she began asking us, "Are you married?" We responded, giggling with the delighted, embarrassed laughter of little girls aching to grow up. It was her way of engaging us in a little adult conversation. She entertained us, enjoyed us, and we returned the favor. But the best part of the visit came after dinner. The men would retreat to the living room in winter or leave the apartment for some fresh air in summer while the women cleared the table and returned to it to talk among themselves. The girls washed the dishes as expected, but Aunt Pauline always helped. I never knew if she was escaping the sisters, cousins, great aunts, brothers, or husbands, but she always pitched in, her hands immersed in soapsuds, washing while I rinsed and dried, and the younger cousins carried dishes, glassware, pots, and pans to the kitchen table to be put away.

"You girls do a really good job," she complimented us. "Better than Fred."

"Uncle Fred does dishes?" I said aloud, speaking for all three of us wide-eyed girls.

"He's a sweet ole man. Make sure you choose a man like him."

"I didn't know men wash dishes. My daddy don't do it," said Renee.

"Yeah, Daddy don't do it," repeated Deidre.

"Daddy doesn't do it," Pauline corrected.

"He doesn't? Then how come Uncle Fred does?"

Pauline threw her head back and laughed.

"Lord have mercy. We've got work to do," she said. "We better start with proper English. You've got plenty of time to learn about men."

"Yeah. Mama always says, 'Pauline sure knows her men!'" I said, anx-

M. Cecile Forte

ious to give my favorite aunt a compliment. "Yes, not yeah, Cecile. Yes, I sure do know my men," she laughed, harder this time, tears forming at the corners of her eyes. That was the start of Aunt Pauline's School of Boys and Men.

Aunt Pauline wasn't a beauty; she didn't have a nice shape, nor luxurious locks. After a time, she wore wigs like all the older women in the family. Furs, custom-made suits, and a hint of lace were her signature. Daddy would say she had "piano-bench legs" whenever he complimented Mama on having the best legs in the family. Once when I was listening outside their bedroom door, Mama said something funny: "It's what's between those legs that counts." I puzzled about why that counts. Why did it count? What did it count for? Who counted it? I wondered. And what does it have to do with piano bench legs, the best legs, or any other legs? Those were questions I saved for Aunt Pauline.

That July, when I came in after play, Mama said, "I have a surprise for you. Pauline called and said she wants you to come stay with her and Uncle Fred for the weekend. It's the Fourth, so you have three days to be with them."

"What about Deedee and Reeney?" I asked.

"She just wants you. You know Pauline can't handle you three. You'll be all by yourself. You don't seem excited."

"Oh, Mama, I am," I said. "I thought you'd say no."

"Why's that?"

"Well, when I wanted to go and she wanted me to come, you always said no."

"Cecile, you're eleven now. That's old enough."

"What about Daddy? Is it okay . . . ?"

"Don't you worry about your daddy. I'll take care of him."

It took time for it to sink in. Me in that beautiful apartment with the French provincial furniture, big mirrors on the wall, candles on the table, the bathroom decorated with a wallpaper filled with roses, a cover on the toilet lid with silk roses on it, a waffle iron, popcorn popper, and the view!

My aunt Pauline gave me a little piece of heaven that weekend. Friday night we spent with Uncle Fred. That was because he was happiest at home, and so were we.

Uncle Fred cooked dinner: roast beef, mashed potatoes, gravy, string beans, rolls, and salad. It was like a restaurant. We popped popcorn and listened to Sarah Vaughan, Ella Fitzgerald, Dinah Washington, Dizzy Gillespie, Cab Calloway, and Count Basie. I knew the music because Daddy was a jazz fan and spent every Saturday night at the Savoy or Small's Paradise after he turned sixteen.

I felt so grown up. They praised me, complimented me, and let me stay up as long as I wanted. That night I fell asleep looking out the window at City College's campus as Uncle Fred lamented the construction of the Engineering Building that would eliminate the view I had been enjoying.

The next morning Aunt Pauline woke me waving two tickets for *Jamaica!*, a musical starring Lena Horne and Ricardo Montalban. I was not myself. I had never seen a Broadway play. We'd done plays in school, so I knew what a play was, but a play on Broadway! I fell asleep and woke up a rich kid! What do you wear to Broadway anyway?

"Aunt P, this is all I have." I showed her: sundresses, shorts, blouses. "I did bring my patent-leather Sunday shoes."

"I think this adventure deserves a new outfit," Aunt Pauline said, "Don't you?"

"Yes, ma'am. Anything you say, Aunt Pauline."

We went shopping at Blumstein's, where my aunt Thelma worked, so we got a 10 percent discount just because she worked there. We found the most beautiful red-plaid sleeveless A-line dress with a belt to match. Aunt Pauline said red was my color. She bought me red shoes with a Cuban heel and taught me how to walk in them. I was so clumsy that I needed help to walk in a one-and-a-half-inch heel! That didn't seem to bother Aunt Pauline, and so it didn't bother me.

We rode an air-conditioned bus back to the apartment, got dressed up, pranced around for Uncle Fred, and then headed for Broadway. We took a taxi to the theater district and walked around a bit, waiting for the three P.M. matinee. We visited with a friend of Aunt Pauline's, a tall, handsome man who looked as if he never got his hands dirty. For some reason, he reminded me of Uncle Fred even though he didn't look anything like him. It took about a year for me to figure out why: Aunt

M. Cecile Forte

115

Pauline behaved differently around men. Her conduct around Larry reminded me of her conduct around Uncle Fred, the softness of her voice, the way she handled her body, crossing her legs and leaning in as if she needed to be closer to hear what Larry said, smiling and touching her hand to her hair. At the time, I was mesmerized by the beauty of the experience and nothing else. He offered to pick us up after the show and take us to the Hotel Theresa for drinks and dinner. I never heard of "drinks and dinner," and I never heard of Broadway either, so I just rode the wave of my ignorance. Adult conversations I overheard long after that meeting clued me in to Larry's place in Pauline's life.

The show? The music, the colors, the sheer beauty of it was awesome. When it was over, Aunt Pauline knew a seamstress who helped get us backstage. I still have Lena Horne's autograph. I will never forget my first musical. The experience made an indelible impression, and Broadway has become a habit, thanks to Aunt Pauline.

Larry drove us to the Hotel Theresa. Aunt Pauline said that Fidel Castro, the president of Cuba, was coming to stay there. I was too young to appreciate why he would stay in that particular hotel.

I slurped the last of my Shirley Temple and began eating the sweet fruity, coconutty confection of ambrosia placed before me. My dinner of salmon tasted nothing like Mama's salmon croquettes, so I picked at it until dessert was served. The peach melba was Larry's very good idea. I finished the whole thing and waited while Larry took care of the bill. When he dropped us off on 143rd Street, he said, "Enjoy your aunt Pauline. She's a special lady." Did he really think I didn't know that?

Sunday morning came too quickly. Aunt Pauline and Uncle Fred took me to Mother Zion Church, where my great-grandmother and grandmother and all my great aunts had worshipped since they came to New York from Jamesville, North Carolina. Nearly all of them were gone. Their daughters took their places in the pews. Even as a child, I could feel their presence and understood the importance of continuity. Most of my family is female. Two generations of girls produced a curiosity about men that took different forms. Though they all got married, most had more male friends than female. A few studied them, certain they could conquer them, and they all loved them, especially Pauline.

On the last night of the weekend, we spent it together in her bedroom, lying across the bed as the air conditioner cooled the room.

"Aunt Pauline, can I ask you a question?"

"May I ask you a question."

"May I . . . Why do people say it's what's between your legs that counts?"

She paused, competing thoughts running through her head. She began with, "CeCe, baby, people say lots of things that have to be interpreted. Can you tell me where you heard this or who said it?"

"Mama said it to Daddy," I told her.

"All right, here goes," she said. "It means that it doesn't matter what a woman looks like or her legs look like, it's the power of the triangle that counts."

"What's that?"

"That's what you call your privates, but the proper names are labia, clitoris, and vagina."

"Who counts your privates?" I asked.

"No one actually counts anything. Counts means what's important."

"But why is it important?"

"Baby, I'm so glad you asked me that question. Do you know that you have been given a gift from God. He chose you and every woman as a cocreator. That gift is carrying a child in your body, feeling a living being moving with life and created to become a healthy, loving individual like yourself. He also gives you wisdom. And you must protect and respect the power of the triangle with that wisdom."

"How?" I asked.

"The only way you can do that is by respecting yourself, thinking about this gift you have. You must only share your gift with someone who values it in the same loving way you do."

"Mama says sex is bad and boys are bad, too."

"Do you think your daddy's bad or Uncle Fred is bad?"

"No, but they're grown-up men, not boys."

"You're absolutely right. Another gift you have is the wisdom to make boys into men."

"I don't know how to do that, Aunt P!"

M. Cecile Forte

"I'll teach you," Aunt Pauline said. "That's what I do best."

Aunt Pauline kept her promise. She shared the mysteries of love, romance, and sex with all of her nieces. She relied on what she called "wisdom of the ages" to help us become appealing, confident young women who know our value and never sell it short. We became adoring women adored by men, Pauline's ultimate compliment. Her openness set us free.

A Toast to Aunt Rose

YANICK RICE LAMB

For the first time in my life, and five days after the end of hers, I was ticked off at Aunt Rose. It wasn't really anger—for who could ever stay mad at Aunt Rose? Or get mad in the first place? It was more akin to the feeling of being on the wrong end of the Dozens. The way you feel when a bid whist opponent has the card to stop you from running a Boston—or worse, when you get taken there. Simply put, I'd been had. Even in death, Aunt Rose had pulled another fast one on me. And all I could do was smile through my tears.

I dabbed my eyes with a balled-up Kleenex from my pocket and was tempted to dig for my glasses. But for what? I clearly saw what I didn't believe I was seeing. The plaque on the satin lining of Aunt Rose's casket read 1893–1994. Aunt Rose hadn't been in her eighties or even in her nineties. She had been 101. I stood in disbelief for what seemed like an eternity.

So, had she told me a story, a tall tale, or a flat-out lie? She'd probably say that she had just led me to believe what I believed. Looking back, I probably got sucked into thinking I knew her real age when I had accompanied her on a doctor's visit not far from her studio apartment in New York. You'd have thought I had discovered the Holy Grail when she gave her age as eighty-two. In reality, she had shaved off roughly a decade to boost her chances of receiving proper health care. I thought it was pretty cool to have been running in and out of stores in midtown Manhattan with a spry chick in her eighties; little did I know that I had been, in fact, hanging out with a prankster in her nineties.

When I recounted all of this to my mother and my aunt Mary, who stepped in as matriarch of the Ford-Jordan clan after my third grandmother and Aunt Rose's sister, Callie Jordan, died in 1977, I felt out of the loop. "Oh yeah," Aunt Mary said. "Aunt Rose turned one hundred last year. We even had a little birthday party for her." It was yet another reminder of the downside of living away from home—missing the markers of life from the cradle to the grave that everyone assumes everyone else already knows. It was also surprising that all of this slipped by me, since I made it a point to visit Aunt Rose whenever I was in Akron and became annoyed at those who couldn't give me an update when I wasn't. How could you not visit Aunt Rose? I always wondered.

Visiting Aunt Rose was the treat of the end of our road trips from Ohio through the tunnels carved out of the Allegheny Mountains in Pennsylvania; the Monopoly-board streets of the *real* Atlantic City; and the cultivated chaos of New York City. We looked forward to visits with Aunt Rose as much as we craved the saltwater taffy that our stepfather, Charles, bought us on the boardwalk after a day collecting seashells on New Jersey's seashore. We were fascinated by her neat and sparsely furnished studio apartment on West 120th Street off Manhattan Avenue, with its busy stoop and bathroom down the hall. It was such a contrast from the one- and two-story houses back home with grassy devil's strips lining the sidewalks and huge maples or weeping willows in the yards. Mostly, though, we were fascinated by Aunt Rose, who had such an affinity for children despite never bearing any of her own. With Aunt Rose, children could be seen *and* heard. She seemed genuinely interested in what we had to say and what we wanted to do. She'd get all up in your business without seeming nosy. She'd tease you to death. She'd get you told.

But as much as she loved to talk, you could never get a straight answer out of her when it came to age. "I'm older than my teeth and younger than my gums," she'd reply to creatively fashioned questions from any of her zillion nieces and nephews. An I-know-something-you-don't-know look of smugness enveloped her face, as her smile and the glint in her eye grew. Her long lean legs would be crossed just so, her top foot bobbing up and down to a rhythm all her own as she savored a sip of sherry.

In the fourth grade, I almost missed our pilgrimage to Aunt Rose's place. I had stepped on a needle trapped in the pumpkin-colored carpet of the bedroom that I shared with my sister, Michelle. I retrieved one piece of the broken needle, and another remained embedded in the carpet. Despite the excruciating pain, I didn't realize that a third piece had made its way into the bottom of my right foot. I kept the incident from my mother until I could no longer walk and found myself on an operating table at Children's Hospital. I quickly learned to maneuver on crutches and begged and begged to head east on our family vacation. While I couldn't navigate Atlantic City's sandy beaches on crutches, I hopped on Manhattan's buses and hobbled down subway stairs under Aunt Rose's watchful eye. She scolded my sister for being impatient and nearly making me lose my balance.

As I grew older, I could visit Aunt Rose on my own and have her all to myself. I enjoyed our girl talk, even though she had a knack for skirting around details. Take "the one who made the earth stand still." To this day, I don't know who he was, when he was in her life, or for how long. But the extra-special glint in her eyes told me more than her words could ever say. The one thing I knew for sure was that I had to have a love like that some day.

Over time, it became clear that Aunt Rose had mad game. She could school you on the ways of the world, the ins and outs of the street, history, music, sports, you name it. She was in her element in New York, a far cry from Midway, Alabama, where she was the eldest of Frances and Porter Ford's eight children. It was no surprise that she moved north at eighteen in the early 1900s after a short stint in Georgia. Aunt Rose was different from all of her sisters—more urban than country, more worldly than domesticated, more interested in completing her education than in settling for the separate-and-unequal instruction that often stopped in primary school in the segregated South. "She was like a modern woman of today," Aunt Mary explains. "She was a go-getter."

Aunt Rose left in search of opportunity, like many black southerners at the front end of the Great Migration. She also left mad as hell after her intended got someone else pregnant and found himself saying "I do" in a shotgun wedding. No one really knows whether she ever married. In New York, she fended for herself, making a living as a seamstress by drawing on skills perfected in her youth. Standing nearly six feet tall and lean as a pole, she always made most of her clothes so that they'd be long enough to drape her body. She dressed simply, yet tastefully, with her thinning gray hair pulled back or curled under. She had an air of confidence that probably served her well when she was running things as a supervising seamstress or putting management in check as a union organizer in the International Ladies Garment Workers. She "retired" after sixty-five years as a garment worker, but she never really sat still.

During an internship in New York the summer after my junior year, I almost went to see jazz singer Alberta Hunter at the Cookery in Greenwich Village. Aunt Rose later told me that she had been on *To Tell the Truth* with Hunter. She was on the verge of a clean sweep of the winnings, having fooled the celebrity questioners into thinking that she was Hunter. However, she was a vote short by the time the announcer said, "Will the real Alberta Hunter please stand up?" According to Aunt Rose, Hunter had revealed too many insider details. "Alberta, you talk too much," Aunt Rose told her. "I could have won this thing!"

On two occasions, Aunt Rose became a surrogate parent, taking in a relative and an adopted goddaughter. She later gave me and my cousin Dennis an orientation on the Big Apple after we relocated there and began working at *The New York Times*. "You know how to read," she declared. "Get a map, and use it! Don't trust anyone—not even the police. Quit laughing. It ain't funny!" My eyebrows were raised, but I tested out her advice and followed it. In my street polls, I'd ask random New Yorkers for directions to well-known intersections and landmarks. Some did, in fact, attempt to lead me astray. As we parted, I'd even hear some people justify their actions by muttering: "That's what they get for asking me. Get on my damn nerves!" I didn't have the heart to test the men and women in blue, potentially adding low marks to disturbing reports of excessive force on unarmed brothers and trigger-happy fingers that mowed down someone's grandmother. So I read the maps. When I came up the wrong set of stairs at a subway stop, I'd keep walking until I reached a bodega, buy gum or a newspaper, and then reverse directions. Aunt Rose would have been proud.

If Aunt Rose's apartment had been bigger, I would have asked to move in and share or take over the rent. After I found out that my great-uncle was relocating his sister near his home in Akron, Ohio, I wished that I had. I wished that I had gotten a larger place and moved her in with me. She was gone before I knew it, her apartment relinquished and her belongings moved to a senior citizens building in downtown Akron. She complained that Akron was too slow. Understanding Aunt Rose, I understood what she meant. Akron was a great place to grow up in, to raise kids in, and to grow old in—except if your name is Rose McKinard.

I'd occasionally bring copies of *The Amsterdam News, The City Sun,* or one of the New York dailies when I'd visit. She'd offer me some sherry—a bottle still on a table near her favorite chair—while peppering me with questions about my life and especially her beloved city. Aunt Rose missed New York, and New York missed her. It didn't matter that she was no longer caught up in its hustle and bustle, that she was asleep when it wasn't. Aunt Rose was one of those people who gave New York its energy. Hell, she gave *life* its energy. She often made me wonder if sherry had any medicinal or life-enhancing properties. But Aunt Rose's real secret was that she was forever young at heart. She enjoyed a good laugh. She saw her glass of sherry as half full, never half empty. She loved life, and it loved her back.

When I see rays of light peeking through the clouds, I know it's the glint from Aunt Rose's eyes. I can just see her chillin' up in heaven with her legs crossed, commiserating with God and my posse of angels. Some of my blessings have her name written on them because she's put in a good word for me.

So here's a toast to you, Aunt Rose. I want to be like you when I grow up.

Yanick Rice Lamb

Role Models

A Gift Given Is a Gift Received

DOROTHY LAZARD

It started innocently enough. I went to the store for her a few times.
Then I was called over to pull weeds or cut fabric for a quilt. All seduc-
tions begin innocently.

When I was twelve, my aunt Mariah was already ancient. She was
my grandmother's older sister, who, like all my close maternal relations,
had moved to California from Chicago. But where the others were irre-
trievably urban, Aunt Ri, as we called her, was deeply rooted in her native rural Arkansas. She settled in a little clapboard cottage in East
Oakland, around the corner from my family. In those days, we were a
large extended family, operating on a strict elder-child model. So when
an elder needed a chore done, a child came. Because of my proximity to
Aunt Ri, and being the youngest, I was usually the one summoned.

She was an odd old lady. She lived alone—few elderly black women
did in those days—so I assumed she was widowed, like my grandmother
had been. When she arrived in California, she was a distant memory for
many on my rung of the family tree; I vaguely remembered a high mahogany bed with a luxurious crocheted throw at its foot, and in the center of the bed, near the pillows, sat a doll, all prim and proper in hoop
skirt and petticoats. Any movement toward this doll would elicit "get
out of there" from Aunt Ri, no matter where she happened to be in the
house. That was my only memory of her, a shadowy scold from the past.

Like her sister, Aunt Ri dipped snuff and always had a coffee can full
of brown sludge that needed emptying. When I went over there, my
plan was always to run to the store, get what she wanted, make sure I
counted the change before returning, drop off the merchandise, and get

out of there fast. I always thought, Maybe she'll forget about the can this time. She never did.

"And don't forget my snuff can," she'd say just before I managed to escape.

The more I was called over, the more I got used to being there. Her home was chock-full of intriguing things. She had a little vanity table, old calendars from funeral homes on the walls, and more china than she'd ever use. She had a variety of mismatched plates with hotel insignias, crocheted doilies, and porcelain knickknacks. On the kitchen wall hung a cat-shaped clock with enormous blinking eyes that scanned the room like searchlights. In the sunroom, jelly jars of plant cuttings rooting in water lined the windows, creating a veiny mosaic. Just as you stepped into the house, there was a sepia-toned photograph of a beautiful young woman dressed in a smart suit like the ones Rosalind Russell or Barbara Stanwyck wore on the late show. I always felt the woman was in the room with us, staring plaintively.

One day on my way out, I asked Aunt Ri about her. "Who is she?"

"That's my daughter."

"Does she live in Chicago?"

"No, she doesn't live anywhere. She's dead."

I was too afraid to ask how such a pretty woman had come to die, although I really wanted to know. I looked at Aunt Ri seated in her living room chair, her snuff can at her feet.

After a time, she said: "She got hold of that narcotic. That narcotic killed her. She's been dead a long time."

I don't remember whether I asked her daughter's name, if I said sorry, or even if that was what I felt at the time, but from that day on Aunt Ri never had to ask me to visit. There was something about her loss (my grandmother had died only a few months before) and her ability to carry on under the weight of it that compelled me to come back. I returned week after week, not so much to comfort her—I didn't think I knew how—but to watch how she kept going. I came on my own, and together we developed a nice routine.

Aunt Ri had a patch of land next to her cottage, about four feet wide and twelve feet long, where she planted tomatoes, potatoes, turnips, and a variety of greens. Her kitchen served as a seed lab, where she had potato plants, avocados, and other things rooting in chipped teacups or jars of water before transplanting them to the yard. She had a country wisdom that I thought had been lost on the road somewhere between Arkansas and California. From the old school of gardening, she had learned cultivation techniques by tradition and experimentation. She never talked of chemical fertilizers or soil mixes. Everything she used was from the earth. I watched quizzically as she threw dried fish bones in the ground along with seeds. If a plant hanging over or poking between the pickets of a fence caught her eye, she'd snip off a sprig or two for herself. With her I experienced for the first time the wonder of biting into a ripe, fresh-off-the-vine tomato, its spray giving me a thousand notions of how things should be.

Despite her age, Aunt Ri was always busy. While we gardened, pots boiled in the kitchen, pies baked in the oven, greens soaked in the sink. There was a sensuousness about the way she lived: alone but so close to wonderful smells, tastes, and textures. Together we cut old shirts, tablecloths, dresses, and pants into squares to make quilts. Textured polyester pants, terry-cloth towels, ripply seersucker shifts—my hands ran across all of these fabrics and across the decades that separated us.

Every girl down south knows how to quilt, she told me. "You take everything you can spare, all your tore-up pants, your aprons, your old work shirts, and you make yourself a quilt. That way nothing goes to waste."

Her south didn't sound as scary as the nightly news made it out to be. It sounded nice, like a place you could learn things and get by using your wits and common sense. I got the sense that Aunt Ri missed the South, her home, but not as much Chicago, where she had most recently lived. Aunt Ri was a great companion. With her I discovered—no, remembered—that I liked using my hands, creating something you could stand back and look at. When I was younger, my mother had taught me to make potholders using scrap fabric and place mats by interfacing silver chewing gum wrappers. But now my mother was sick a lot, and she had let her hobbies go.

Dorothy Lazard

I told Aunt Ri about my homemaking classes, how we were learning to use the new Singer sewing machine, but she scoffed at such modern technology.

"Your hands are what's best," she'd mutter.

At Aunt Ri's house I was trying to escape the social pressures of the world outside. I was in what would later be described as a "weird space," not fully comfortable with being a teenager. Not ready to be hip or boy-crazy. Youth was always too much of a mob scene to me. Too much groupthink, not enough freedom of expression. At home, the pressure was unspoken. I was living with my chronically ill mother and two older siblings—who loved me dearly—but were both too young to provide me with the parenting I needed. Aunt Ri's house was neutral ground. In exchange for some labor, I found a place where I could just be. I didn't have to talk or perform or impress or explain. I could just absorb what was around me. There was no monitoring my mother's seizures or fighting with my brother over whether we'd watch *The Rookies*, or something equally mundane on TV. There was no hallway gossip or after-school fistfights or nauseating flirtations.

I got to know Aunt Ri as much as she would let anyone know her. She introduced me to her old-lady friends who lived in two houses directly across the street. They didn't seem as old or alone in the world as Aunt Ri. They had visiting children and grandchildren. They were a chatty, busy, and generous bunch. They stuffed me with greens and corn bread and sweet potato pies, and when I said "No, thanks," they simply took that to mean I'd take some home. And off they'd go, rushing for the plastic containers and aluminum foil.

My favorite thing to do was to visit Aunt Ri on Sunday afternoon. We'd garden a bit, cook dinner together (peeling potatoes was my specialty), and, at six o'clock sharp, seat ourselves in front of the TV to have dinner and watch *The Tom Jones Show*. My aunt Mariah loved Tom Jones. It was the strangest thing. On the surface, she was this cantankerous old woman who was at the end of her life. But let Tom Jones show up, and she was like my sister with Smokey Robinson, or me with Michael Jackson. She was a giggly, breathless teenager. I always wondered what this "blue-eyed soul brother" (from Wales, of all places) would make of my elderly great-aunt, all wide hips and false teeth. She was convinced he had some black blood.

"No full-white man can dance like that," she'd declare. "And look at his hair . . . how kinky it is," she would add as further evidence.

I already learned not to talk with Aunt Ri about anything having to do with race. She was very old-fashioned about it. Whenever the subject of Africa came up, which it usually did with my older sister, Sarah, Aunt Ri would swear that she was not African and would have nothing to do with the term *Afro-American*. She was a Negro, and, as far as she was concerned, so was Tom Jones.

There was no talking during the program, no crossing in front of the TV for a dinner roll, no singing along to "Delilah." Absolute silence was required.

"He *is* a good-looking man," she'd exclaimed over her dinner plate. "Look at how he's wearing those pants. My goodness."

Tom Jones was pretty entertaining, certainly better than Dean Martin slurring over his cocktail, but I can't say I watched him very closely. I was too busy watching *her* watch him. And like clockwork, each week before he performed his signature "It's Not Unusual" sign-off song, Aunt Ri, seventy-five, if she was a day, would ask with all the earnestness and anticipation the human heart could muster: "Do you think his pants are going to split this week?"

I didn't really look forward to that happening, but I was fascinated that she was. Every week I said I didn't know. Jones's pants were so tight they looked like a second skin. But I said I didn't know because I wanted to leave a little room for dreaming.

My last clear memory of seeing Aunt Ri was at my mother's funeral in 1972. After the service I sat numb and alone in the back of the funeral home's limousine. My brother and sister mingled with the rest of the family. I wanted to walk home, to get away from the mourning, from the church where my mother's body lay—the last place I would see her. Besides, it seemed ridiculous to ride in such a grand car to a church around the corner. Aunt Ri and her friends approached me tentatively. I got out of the car to greet them.

"You poor girl," one of them said.

The others nodded. They held my hand in theirs, rubbed my arm, my cheek. Then Aunt Ri, the ambassador of the group, stepped closer to me.

"You can come live with me if you want to," she said. "We can take care of you." She tipped her head toward her friends.

I didn't know how to respond. I was moved. I was scared. What would my life be like living among three elderly women? Where would I sleep in her tiny cottage? When could I play my records or look at late-night movies? I thought of her old hands quilting.

How would our relationship, which had been so easy, so fruitful, change if I lived with her? I thought of her lost daughter. How would my sister and brother feel if I left them? Because my mother had been sick my entire life, I had been moved around so much. With my sister, Sarah, I could stay put, stay at the same school for more than a year or two.

"No," I finally said. "Thank you, though. I'll be okay."

"Well, if you need anything, you let us know," my aunt Ri said.

"Don't be a stranger," said one of her friends.

"No, ma'am, I won't."

Then Aunt Ri and her entourage left.

I don't have much memory of Aunt Ri after my mother's funeral. The next year, before I began ninth grade, Sarah and I moved to West Oakland to a nice, new apartment, roomier than what we were used to. My brother, grieving for our mother, moved to Chicago. Aunt Ri eventually moved back, too. She had cousins and old friends there. The California relations always seemed more my grandmother's clan than hers. In the times when I wasn't doing homework, watching TV, obsessing about boys, trying to fit in with girls, discovering new interests, and adapting to Sarah as my legal guardian, I would think of Aunt Ri and how pleasant it had been to be with her. She hadn't asked much of me but taught me so much. She died sometime when I was in college.

These days I think of Aunt Ri a lot. She was a role model for me in more ways than she ever realized. From her, I learned that it was absolutely fine to live alone. With few other models of female independence, Aunt Ri taught me that a woman could thrive keeping her own company. She was born poor and died poor, but parts of her life were so rich with interests and activity. Having spent most of my adulthood single and without children, I've gotten a chance to see life from Aunt Ri's perspective. Although we were born in vastly different times with vastly different opportunities, Mariah and I each found the space and time to look inside ourselves and to appreciate what we saw.

I see her legacy in my garden, a quarter-acre in urban Oakland. Each year I plant a variety of tomatoes and collard greens in her honor. As I stand in the garden, plucking tomatoes from the vine and eating them like apples, I remember the miracle of that first bite into a homegrown tomato in her yard—its taste, its spray filling me with possibilities. I take pride in the food I raise and in seeing people I love enjoy that food. I recycle like the law is after me, looking at everything for any dual purpose it might have. And while I never took to quilting like Aunt Ri would have wanted me to, I'm a fiendish knitter, going so far as to unravel old sweaters to make new garments. My house, like my aunt's, is a carnival of mismatched furniture and dishes, half-finished craft projects, seed jars, and snipped plants rooting in water.

I attribute my calling to mentor young people to her. I've been a librarian, a teacher, a tutor, and a student adviser. I've passed on my enthusiasm for gardening, writing, film, and books to the young people around me. But, most important, I've been a dedicated aunt to my brother's children, and that, I'd like to think, would make my Aunt Ri most proud. She taught me I didn't have to be a mother to mother someone. I didn't have to have money or status to share what I have. I came to reevaluate my relationship with my great-aunt when I became the steadying force in my niece's and nephew's lives. What I gave to them was returned to me so many times over that I now feel any gift given is a gift received. The opportunity to be in a child's life—to nourish, to guide, to learn from them—is such a profound endeavor. Children need to see that people other than their parents are concerned about them and interested in them. From those seemingly tangential relationships children can learn other ways of being and new ways of looking at the world. My aunt taught me that I was my community's child and that one day I would be responsible for passing along its gifts. This is Mariah's legacy.

Dorothy Lazard

Patchwork of Love

ANGELA DODSON

Nearly every day someone in my family takes a thick quilt to snuggle up for a nap or to sit quietly in the den for an evening of television. We know that it probably should be framed or stored in museum-quality wrapping, but here our quilts are used the way they were intended by the loving hands that stitched them. Even when I try to set them aside as "art," displayed on a bent-twig quilt rack, a guest is likely to borrow one for warmth in the middle of the night.

Authentic, handmade quilts have always been in abundance in our home. Most are gifts from aunts long passed on and reflect my Appalachian heritage and my husband's Gullah ancestors. My favorite aunt, Ida, made a pink one for our wedding more than twenty years ago. Ida Mae Walthall Towns, my mother's eldest sister, is still quilting to this day from her room in a nursing home at the age of eighty-four. Nearly a decade after she sent the wedding gift, my husband rediscovered the quilt, anointed this one as the warmest in the house, and restored it to a place in the family room.

Aunt Ida's quilts are not the complex ones with tiny stitches and intricate patterns that intimidate the everyday person. They are thick and homey with big patches and clumps of knotted threads that are easier on her arthritic hands.

Even as a little girl, I remember quilts arriving regularly in the mail from Aunt Ida in North Carolina, usually when a family member reached a milestone—or just because. Even when quilts fell out of vogue for a while, they were still revered in our family.

When Aunt Ida moved into the nursing home years ago, we assumed her gifts of quilts would stop. They didn't. When my brother, Bill, and I visited her in her tiny room there, we found her surrounded by stacks of fabric and finished quilts, her sewing machine at hand. Aunt Ida's room is also filled with photographs of her many grandchildren, great-grandchildren, as well as nieces and nephews, who are scattered around the country, as if to remind her where her quilts went. While other residents watch television or play cards and checkers, Aunt Ida sews.

A year or so ago, Ida asked her son, Jan, to store her sewing machine and supplies at his home in South Carolina while she was recovering from an illness, but a few months later she cheerfully called me to report that she had them back up and running.

If age has slowed her pace, it doesn't show in her quilting. For most of her life, Ida has endured a severe weight problem as far back as I can remember. Aunt Ida tried everything, including visiting some of the best medical programs in the country, but other health issues complicated the treatment. She never seemed to mind when we took her to the freight station during our visits for weighing, but she did chafe a bit when my father, with his keen wit, methodically calculated exactly where she should sit in his new car for proper balance. I once heard her tell a child trying to climb up on her for a hug: "No, baby, Grandma doesn't have any lap." Everybody knew her weight was dangerous, but Ida has outlived many of her slimmer relatives by decades, including my mother.

We all learned long ago to accept that Ida was also epileptic and has a speech impediment or pattern in which she throws a strange series of syllables into nearly every sentence. If you don't know her, it can make listening to her very difficult. If you do, the sound of her voice is a source of great comfort and a little amusement. Every few weeks she calls if she hasn't heard from any of us. The calls became more frequent after Mother died in the early 1980s.

She is renowned for her quilts and beloved by her former neighbors. People from around her former home in Macon, North Carolina, would come by to purchase her work and take her to church. Although she charges little for the quilts, she carefully signs each one. When Aunt Ida runs low on supplies, the neighbors and friends come to take her to the store or one of the many fabric outlets to buy notions and fabric for

Angela Dodson

more quilts. As a leader in senior citizen causes for many years, she has many friends, and her quilts are well known throughout the surrounding area.

A few years ago my brother persuaded Aunt Ida to make a quilt from his old T-shirts, preserving their various slogans and memories. As he described the end product over the phone, I couldn't imagine what such a quilt would look like, but when he brought his for me to see one Christmas, I knew I had to have one, too. I gathered up my T-shirts and sent them off to her. Within about two weeks, I got back not one, but two commemorative quilts. With no direction from me, she had carefully sorted my life into its professional side with shirts from various journalism events and a more personal one, filled with things like family trees from the reunions of both my parents' clans to political slogans—all backed with charming cotton prints and quilted with the usual hand-tied knots.

All of my aunt Ida's quilts are like living scrapbooks. The earlier ones came not only bearing her love, but that of her sister, Kira Evelyn Walthall Dodson, the middle child of five, who was my mother. She was a gifted seamstress whose beautiful dresses live on in the fabric scraps she supplied. Every now and then, I can glimpse a patch made from a plaid dress I wore in first grade or a pink-flocked piece of one of mother's Jackie Kennedy–inspired Sunday dresses circa 1960.

The quilts stir up memories of watching my mother and her sisters sew, or of tagging along to the "pieced goods" stores where an infinite rainbow of colors and the fresh scent of just-loomed cotton flooded my senses. In that world, a little girl's wardrobe was limited only by the imagination. Frugality and practicality in those days dictated that every inch of fabric left over was passed on to a quilter.

Trading fabric led to a trip to visit Aunt Ida. Back then my family lived mostly in western or central Pennsylvania and Aunt Ida in North Carolina, her husband's home state. Every other year or so, Will Dodson, my father, would drive nearly a day to take Mom to visit her beloved eldest sister. Bags and bags of scraps would be packed onto the station wagon along with the luggage. One year when people kept waving and pointing at our car, Mom and Pop thought they were admiring their new 1959 Chevrolet Impala wagon, the long, silvery blue one with wings. Miles down the road we all realized that brightly colored rags had been zipping off the top of the Chevy, creating quite a Beverly Hillbilly's–type spectacle.

Rural North Carolina seemed like a trip back in time. My aunt and her husband, C.T., lived in small cabins, usually adjoining someone's farm, with no neighbors in direct sight. They would place a red bandana in the doorway to help us find their tiny house along the road. Until I was an adult, Ida had no indoor plumbing, but I hardly noticed the in-convenience. Everything about our vacation there fascinated me. We could ride mules, pick melons from the vine, fish in a huge lake all day, and buy pickles out of a jar at the country store. Her church held huge suppers out in a field, offering more varieties of fruits and vegetables than I could count. Our outings included day trips to see tobacco being cured or to buy a year's supply of fabric at the nearby cotton mills. We carried home souvenirs of sugarcane or yellow watermelons.

We also carried home our first impressions of public racial segrega-tion. Being from the North, Bill and I had never seen segregation signs until Ida and C.T. took our family to nearby cities in North Carolina. The "white" and "colored" labels intrigued Bill and me more than it re-pelled or surprised us. The notion of "white" and "colored" drinking water was for us an intellectual curiosity and thus fair game for our wicked sense of humor even then. We did not have to live with visible segregation daily. My parents, who had, were not amused, having lived most of their lives under segregation in Virginia and West Virginia.

The West Virginia of my parents' youth sounded much like the Old West frontier. The old folks spun tales of hard work, sacrifice, and perse-verance. They lived well in the early boom years, and then weathered the Depression, the rationing of World War II, and declining fortunes after the war, when thousands of families began to leave West Virginia to find work. From this grew a kind of thrift, adaptability, and range of skills that amazed me.

Ida, Mama, and the other sisters learned to sew as a matter of course, and Grandma Lillie even sold some of her handiwork, mostly beautiful aprons. Louise avoided sewing for years but later made fine appliqué quilts she sold through one of the West Virginia antipoverty programs. All the women made patterns from newspapers and bragged that they

Angela Dodson

could design outfits based on any photograph or drawing in the papers or magazines. Mother and Louise sewed almost literally till they died.

Ida, who rarely travels, rode a bus for the better part of two days to get to Kira's bedside, and her sister's name was one of the last words my mother uttered as she recognized her. It almost seemed that she had waited for Ida's arrival before she could take leave of this world. I don't see her that often anymore, but I send her a little check every Christmas and usually a contribution to her church homecoming, the third Sunday in August. My brother sends her a gift on our mother's birthday.

Every day the quilts recall Ida's love for all of us. We were reminded recently when my eldest son got married that the circle remains un-broken. In the mail, he got a quilt from Aunt Ida.

A Cool Drink of Well Water

KATHY LYNN HARRIS

I never once saw her wear pants. Always a thin cotton dress, hemmed to
her knees— revealing the purple-veined mosaics on her bare calves and
the scar near her ankle. She finished the ensemble off with old tennis
shoes whose rubber soles were worn thin; she wore no socks. It didn't
matter that she might have spent her days mending barbed-wire fence,
or working a hundred head of cattle, or canning peaches, or pulling
weeds from her garden, or picking dewberries, or driving a John Deere
across three pastures. It just wasn't fitting for a lady to wear pants.

Throughout my childhood, Aunt Deddy was synonymous with two
things for me: the Baker Place and cool well water on a hot, dry, southern Texas day.

Aunt Deddy was my father's aunt; my grandmother's only sister.
She lived on the old family homestead, what we all called the Baker
Place, in the small, dog-run-style home she and my grandmother were
born in. She kept a heck of a garden in the back, which flourished despite the grasshoppers that so commonly invaded the land and popped
in your face as you walked through her yard.

My father runs cattle on the hundred or so acres there, as did my
grandmother before she suffered a debilitating stroke. My family spent
many a Sunday morning and afternoon at the Baker Place, feeding or
working cattle, sometimes fishing in the front tank.

South Texas summers are unmercifully hot. The temperature can
easily climb to ninety-five degrees before ten A.M. The land is dry and
brittle except for two or three months in the spring, and mesquite trees
offer the only speakable shade. When my dad worked cattle, I was often

charged with tossing sections of hay bales during feeding, and standing in a designated spot to keep the cattle going in the right direction when we rounded them to the pens. This, believe it or not, made me incredibly thirsty. And the most comforting thought I can remember from those days was knowing Aunt Deddy was always standing by with a glass of cool water when we were done.

I never liked well water—the sulfur and iron and other sediments never felt quite right as they filled my nose before they bounced against my tongue. But for some reason, on those days, sipped from Aunt Deddy's little tin cups of bright green and blue metallic, it could have been champagne. I imagine now that the reason I wasn't given more important cattle-working tasks was because I couldn't keep quiet or still. Sometimes I didn't even make it into the pasture with Daddy and my older sister. Instead, I was sent to Aunt Deddy's house to visit with her, while all the real fun was happening outside. My little sister came with me, because in those days we were generally a package deal. We'd sit in Aunt Deddy's front living room while box fans hummed in the windows. The warm air from outside mixed inside with the smell of cabbage cooking in the kitchen. I'd stare past her polyester pink curtains to see if I could tell what was going on in the pasture. I'd hope longingly for a few minutes to run through the gullies of the land, free from small talk and the rocking of her chair. We talked some, about the weather, about the family, about the cattle, about her kids and grandkids, sometimes about her sewing or quilting, or our schoolwork and friends. I did love Aunt Deddy's voice with its colorful Texas drawl.

Sometimes we played a few games of Crazy Eight or Wahoo on a wobbly plywood card table to pass the time. I remember her squatting in her cotton dress to play jacks with us on her front porch. The porch, which was built at the turn of the twentieth century, was so uneven that trying to catch the rubber ball was quite a challenge. But the crumbling concrete was shaded, and that meant a cool slab on your legs, and that was worth having to crawl in her rose bushes to find the wayward balls.

Aunt Deddy is gone now; we recently lost her. She lived to be more than ninety years old, only a month of which was spent outside Baker Place. I wish that I had been a little less concerned about what was going on out in the pasture on those hot days, and had listened more intently to the woman who taught us to value the feel of bare legs on a shaded concrete porch.

I know little of her past, really. I asked my father a few questions here and there over time, but it's not our family habit to talk much about the past. I know she never worked away from the Baker Place, never had a job other than working the land she was born on, making her living from cattle and crops. I know she was married only once, and had her children by that same man.

In the stories I've created in my mind, her husband went to prison for some crime, maybe an armed robbery or a murder so awful that she couldn't bear to look at him again. Maybe she found him in the barn with a woman from another county. The truth is, whatever he did to cross her matters less than the fact that she divorced him at a time when divorce was simply unheard of in rural Texas. She chose to lose the man with whom she'd chosen to spend the rest of her life, the one who did at least half the work that kept her family fed. Still, she just carried on, all the time sipping well water in her cotton dress.

I'm in my thirties now and have been through a few personal crises of my own, including a traumatic marriage that didn't make it even close to the happily-ever-after mark. In the months following my divorce, Aunt Deddy wrote to me several times. Her eyesight was beginning to fail her some, but she still wrote. She never mentioned my failed marriage—not once. Instead, our letters were much the same as our small talks when I was a kid: the weather, the family, the land, the pink-and-green quilt she was making for me from one my grandmother had started before her stroke. I wrote back with news of my job, my friends, of when I'd be home next. We didn't need to say more than that. I felt her courage and wisdom with every mention of her daily life.

I think of the pain she must've gone through back then. Realizing her husband was not the man she'd thought he was. Demanding that he leave her family's land. Forcing herself to go on without him. Choosing to spend her life alone. Bearing the whispers and words of a small town. Raising two children on her own in an unforgiving, poverty-stricken rural area. With nothing but the land to save her.

In one of her letters she sent a favorite recipe of hers, one for Mexican Butter Steak—guaranteed, she'd written, to cure a bad day. At the

Kathy Lynn Harris

141

time, I thought it was more likely to harden every artery in my body, so I tucked it away somewhere, thinking perhaps there would come a day when I could brave the four sticks of butter.

I recently found that recipe she sent me, just after another major change in my life. I had just moved from Texas, alone, to another state, where I knew no one. Mexican Butter Steak never tasted so good.

Aunt Deddy's spirit, I believe, is scattered now. In the gullies and coastal grass of the Baker Place. In the creaking hardwood floors of her home. In the black dirt of her garden. In the pots and pans of her kitchen. In the scent of her rosebushes. In her wooden recipe box. In the water we'll continue to drink from the well.

Rice Girls

ONG JEN HONG

Desert Seedlings

Growing up in Arizona, my siblings and I spent our after-school hours at
my grandparents' house, along with the dozen other Chinese neighborhood children whose parents were busy earning an American living. My
aunt Jing governed the gaggle of children with her repertoire of games,
including backyard Red Rover and indoor Simon Says, and a host of
mild threats.

At the time, most of the baby-sitters were adolescent girls, and we
all wanted to be like Jing, a cheerleader in junior high, a pom-pom girl
in high school. She had feathered hair, wore Tickle deodorant, smelled
of Love's Baby Soft, and glossed her lips with a spongy wand that tasted
like bubble gum. She wound our hair into Princess Leia donuts, ran ribbons through our braids. She said braces were cool, and we all took
photographs with strips of aluminum foil crimped across our teeth. She
orchestrated living room beauty pageants and (she told me years later)
always let me win.

We loved hanging out in her bedroom, with the posters of Rick
Springfield and Duran Duran on her walls. To give us some industry as
she took a nap, she let us draw on the soles of her feet with ballpoint
pens: flowers, butterflies, smiley faces, and "Scott Baio loves Jing." Of
course he did. We all did.

She said she was going to be a nurse. I said, "Me, too." Then she
changed her mind. "I'm going to be a fashion designer." "Me, too." "You
always want to be what I want to be." "I do not." She drew us cartoon
puppies and paper dolls, and I reverently copied.

When I spent the night at my grandparents' home, sharing Jing's bed, she tried everything to get me to go to sleep. "Count my hair," she'd command, turning over, and I'd lift the long, straight black strands one by one. "Give me a massage." "Rub lotion into my feet."

Our favorite time of year was spring, when she splayed open her school yearbook and, page by page, had us select the prettiest and the ugliest students. Her yearbook was always full of messages, round, bubbly script written by the popular girls. We loved flipping the pages and seeing her and her friends' faces on every other page: cheerleading, yearbook, dance, student government, National Honor Society. She was the one we hoped to grow up to be.

Until she grew up herself.

I wouldn't understand until I was older how suffocated she felt, forced every day to supervise the children crawling all over the house, not a moment to herself. One day she was our favorite baby-sitter, the next a reclusive hellcat. Though the middle child, Jing was the first child to be raised in America. She wanted the independence her friends had, which drove my non-English-speaking grandparents to despair. They begged my mother to take corrective action, to mold her into the proper Chinese girl she was supposed to be. The more rules they set, the greater her hunger for escape. My aunt's determination to break free coincided with my early adolescence. Without a fun-loving, carefree aunt as a mentor, I turned to the Southern Baptist Chinese Church, where most of Phoenix's Chinese youth went to foster cultural community.

Instead of inheriting Jing's feminine charm and ease, I turned inward, branding everything my classmates did as sin—groping in the hallways, drinking at parties, cheating on homework, avoiding Sunday school. I also feared for the soul of my aunt, who had turned away from the church and chosen to live with a white man, unmarried, no less. She seemed to live the glamorous life, only visiting with her boyfriend at Christmas, taking exotic trips and showering us with expensive gifts on birthdays and holidays. Behind my fragile cheer and gratitude, however, I felt distant from her. She was not the one we were supposed to be like—a harlot and rebel.

Buds

Higher education awakened my feminist spirit and exposed to me the duplicity of my church's values. My drawing skills (initially inspired by Jing) led me into the world of political art, in which I dissected religious repression, sexism, racism, capitalism, feminism, homophobia, etc., with a furrowed brow, pen, and paintbrush. I was as serious a scholar as I had been a Southern Baptist. Aunt Jing's influence on me waned, after I'd entered college, left the church, and started having my own love affairs and art shows. Plus, the family could now see her as a positive influence, having established herself in Los Angeles as a graphic designer and having met a nice Jewish boy who became her fiancé. My grandparents by then had accepted her penchant for tall, blond men and were eager to see her settle down and start having grandchildren.

Jing tried again and again to lure me into commercial illustration and proudly circulated my doodles of leggy fashion models in her advertising office. "You're so talented! Why don't you do something with it?" she pleaded. She supplied me with industry leads, but I was determined to avoid the bewitching influence of advertising. I was still enamored with the idea of myself as an impoverished, solitary artist.

After I graduated from art school, my only passion was to run as far as I could from any degree of normalcy. Jing helped with that. Between jobs and world travels, I visited her three or four times a year and rued my lack of direction. It was always a treat to visit Jing in Los Angeles: Jing, who had escaped the dusty confines of our hometown; Jing, who had created a world of beauty around her. I had worked abroad in several countries but always ended up back in Phoenix broke, living with my parents.

I loved the clean, white walls and furnishings of her apartment, the way sunlight flooded through the windows and spotlighted her elegant arrangements of votive glasses, dried flowers, and black-and-white photographs of herself as a child in Hong Kong. The simple lines, the sparse, bold colors, and the chunky candles releasing their honeyed vanilla scents presented a dreamland of cheerful perfection, so different from our upbringing in dark, cramped homes heavy with the smell of dried fish, shitake mushrooms, and grease.

Her storage habits betrayed her immigrant blood—save everything.

Ong Jen Hong

Grocery sacks and stylish boutique bags brimmed from her cleaning cabinet. Boxes of shoes, many of which she had never worn, took up half her closet. A highly efficient pack rat, she stowed away her favorite eighties clothes neatly in boxes. "Just give them away," I insisted during the annual thinning of her possessions. "You want to give everything away. And you'll miss it when it comes back into fashion," she said as she held out a polka-dotted, triple-tiered, black-and-white miniskirt.

I packed little on my trips to see Jing, as I usually wore the clothes from her closet and bathed with her creamy soaps. Taking a shower was like making a salad, so many scents and volume-boosting, shine-enhancing shampoos from which to choose. I'd emerge from the steaming bathroom smelling of strawberries or pears or lemons, a little bit like my aunt . . . until I started to sweat. "My God, why don't you wear any deodorant?" she'd ask. "And, ew, look at your legs—so hairy, like whiskers! Don't touch me!"

Tall and voluptuous for a Chinese woman, Jing emphasized her assets with platform sandals and snug T-shirts. She carried designer handbags and had Jennifer Aniston hair. I'd tag along with her to her advertising agency, guitar lessons, yoga and kickboxing classes, sushi with her friends, and the grocery store, grim in my combat boots and crew cut.

She loved having me around as a little sister. She'd say, "Forget the Spice Girls. We're the Rice Girls!" I was always amazed at how comfortably Jing wore her Asian skin. For all my study of the Asian diaspora, the Asian American's double-edged identity, and the need for solidarity, I had to admit I had few, if any, Asian friends. She, meanwhile, without spewing any socio-political theory, loved being Chinese, had Asian friends, and even introduced me to my first and only fling with an Asian man (which she warned me from the beginning would not be a good idea. But I was too determined to experience "Asian love" to listen).

Later we pondered how different my life would have been had she been around in my awkward teenage years, as there I was in my mid-twenties, still skittish around men, choosing instead to think I was too smart for anyone. She, of course, could see right through me. "Why do you have to be so angry all the time?" she asked one visit, when I was furious with constipation and the day's procrastinations.

I was very angry at the world. There were so many injustices to correct, minds to enlighten, rain forests to save. If the meek didn't inherit the earth, then I was certain smart people did. I didn't think Jing, with her laughter and simplicity, had anything to teach me. In my mind, I was a feminist; she was female.

Bitter Blossoms

Jing never succeeded in persuading me to pursue an illustration career. Instead I found a haven in the study of acupuncture and homeopathy, and as I began to assist in the healing of individuals' bodies and souls, I felt that my whole family should be able to receive my graces, including Aunt Jing.

She had been having relationship issues for years, and I thought I had the answers. Once again, I invoked the spirit of judgment and self-righteousness. I spouted New Age and pop psychology verbiage, and she mumbled in misery, "I know it's about me and what I want, I know." She could be cruel to the men in her life, a personality trait acquired from her venom-tongued mother. She wanted to stop, but she didn't know how. She wanted to stop fearing abandonment, but she didn't know how. She wanted to be happy with her life and herself, but she didn't know how.

I threw up my hands and gladly relocated to the other side of the country, far from her irresolution. She mourned our separation and with each phone call proposed that the two of us return to our hometown. "I'd move back if you were there. We could start a business together," she said, and claimed she'd be stronger in her relationships and career if she had the support of family. Weary of her weightless plans, I submerged myself into my new life and profession in Atlanta.

A year later, however, I found myself in Jing's shoes, wondering where to go and what to do after completing a physically and emotionally exhausting year in professional healing. "Move back," she urged, but I was stubborn. I was not ready to return home. There were already too many demons to face in my own heart, without bearing the crushing love of blood ties.

I had little time for someone who could not implement my cold,

Ong Jen Hong

147

clear advice to change her life completely. I continued to distance my-self from Jing and turned to my younger sister as a confidante. Each Christmas reunion, I became increasingly annoyed with Jing's vacilla-tions, especially with her volatile relationships and the never-ending question of whether she should move home.

We pitied her. We did not know what had become of the aunt who used to energize the room with her buoyancy. We used to say that her alternately tough and zany personality reminded us of different movie and television characters: Holly Golightly, Jo Polniaczek, Mallory Keaton. We used to revel in baking homemade crackers and staying up all night to talk about our boyfriends, careers, and people who annoyed us. Though we merrily unwrapped her presents, each packaged with Martha Stewart flair, and laughed obligingly at her whimsical nature, we sensed the shadow creeping under her zest for life and resented her chronic tardiness and self-absorption.

In our late-night sessions of *king gai*, or gossip, she told my sister and me about her fears of getting older, of not yet being settled, of not yet having a child, of not being completely comfortable or happy in Los Angeles, of disappointing her parents, of losing her parents, of not being taken care of, of driving her current fiancé away with her moodi-ness. . . . It took everything I had not to lose my temper, but the wrath simmering beneath my skin was obvious.

One night during the holidays, after Jing had left for her parents' home, I curled up in bed with my sister. I groaned, "I've done my medi-tation, tried to be compassionate, tried to see the lesson in all this, but the only way I can stop judging her is to not spend any time with her. Why does she drive me so crazy?"

My sister responded: "Because she reminds you of your own inde-cisiveness."

I paused and wondered.

Fruition

I've learned that Jing and I are not so different after all. On opposite sides of the country, we fantasize about the books we plan to write, centering on our wonderfully backward family. We learn how to cook traditional Cantonese dishes—*dongs* (sticky rice wrapped in bamboo and lotus leaves), *jook* (rice porridge), *mu choy* (preserved mustard greens), *yow mei fan* (sausage and shitake mushroom–infused rice). We decorate our homes with good luck tangerines for Chinese New Year and let them shrivel up on our shelves. We laugh about our childhoods in Phoenix, how we escaped the Chinese church that would have had us breeding clever, God-fearing children with honorable Chinese men.

Instead, unmarried and childless and shakily self-employed, we disappoint and exhilarate our parents with our shenanigans. We argue with our non-Chinese lovers about money and domestic responsibility. We wonder how to work on our personal creative projects while earning a living. We ache to be closer to our roots at the same time we treasure our independence. We long to make the world a more beautiful place. We realize the importance of healing and loving ourselves, the harvest of being kind, the power of our womanhood, and the power of our kitchens, inherited from mothers whose blood instinct is to feed first, ask questions later.

She calls today, and it is almost like old times, talking about our ambitions and relationships. She is stronger now in knowing who she is and what she wants. For a long time I considered myself smarter and more mature than Jing and didn't think she had anything significant to teach me. In hindsight I see she was the one—more than anyone else in the world—who supported me in all my endeavors, believing in me before I knew how to believe in myself. She never bragged that she was right, never demanded that I do things her way. And she has never, ever been angry with me, despite the ugliness I have heaped upon her.

Sometimes you have to step away from a relationship, or friendship, to allow room for individual growth. It amazes me that it took so many years of education, so many miles of travel, so many pages of books, so many reels of self-help tapes, so many hours of meditation, so many nights of gossip, to see the light glimmering in Jing all along.

There's no place like home.

Thank you, Aunt Jing, for showing me the face of unconditional love.

Ong Jen Hong

Women of Fortitude

ESTHER IVEREM

As we maneuver through this new century and millennium, I feel keenly the sense of a generation passing slowly before my eyes, that last generation of African Americans who lived well into middle age in a country that unapologetically offered them second-class citizenship. I have recently buried two elderly aunts, my father's oldest and surviving sisters—Emma Moore and Bessie Felder Miller. In the process of helping my parents make final preparations for them, I have grappled with what my aunts' lives meant to me.

I never saw my aunts defeated. Even if they were beaten, they were never beat. Whether because of the haze of fast living, or sober practicality, or religious faith, they always beamed at me. Even now, remembering them in their frailer final years, I remember their smiles, their sense of grace and resolution that everything was just fine.

All the sisters—Rosezell, Anna Mae, Bessie, and Emma—are gone now, leaving behind their baby brother, the spoiled temperamental son, my father. Of the four aunts, I was closest to the youngest, Rosezell, whom I called Aunt Rosie. When I was a toddler, she was the light of my life as well as my caretaker while my mother worked in a garment factory. She was a tall, stout woman, with a round, smiling face, who wore her short hair curled neatly away from her face. She was a wonderful cook and baker; her cakes and pies would disappear fastest at family gatherings. In fact, she loved sweets, and I was a young, eager convert to the cult of sugar. In her kitchen, there would be jars of candy waiting. Her sandwiches and Kool-Aid always tasted the best. Once, I watched with wide-eyed amazement as she made a tall stack of glazed doughnuts on top of her stove.

Aunt Rosie worked at night as a nurse so her days were free. We went to the little corner grocery stores in North Philadelphia that were always dark and smelled like Jewish pickles. At a little record store, the counterman would play records for us because Aunt Rosie always knew the tune of the song she wanted to buy but never its name. The walk to her third-floor apartment, and then to the neat brick two-story row house she subsequently purchased, was like an adventure. She even made nap time more bearable by convincing me that if I slept, my stubby plaits would grow longer. It seems now that we spent hours on end in the musty and dusty aisles of Goodwill as she sorted through cast-off clothing, the remainders of dish sets, and appliances that had seen better days.

She loved and had an eye for beautiful furnishings, and she knew that there were plenty of beautiful things discarded by folks every day, which could be had for far less than what things cost in a department store. She and my mother had a code word for Goodwill and other thrift stores. In earshot of others, they would say that they were going "to Wanamaker's," meaning the fancy John Wanamaker department store downtown on Market Street. They carried on this ruse with a wink and a smile so well and for so long that I was often confused about where we were going, and about whether Goodwill was really named Wana-maker's. One day, I saw her pull down an intricately crocheted blanket from a top shelf. I have that blanket now, as well as the colorful dishes she found and used, which I later learned are the now-sought-after Fiestaware. And I have her old couch with carved, wooden feet.

My aunt Rosie had a steady boyfriend, but she never married. And though she never had children of her own, we, her nieces and nephews—many of whom she raised as her own—filled some of that void. She fell into a diabetic coma and died when I was a freshman in college. Her sudden death left me feeling robbed and sad and alone. I knew an important part of my life had just passed away. I wrote her obituary, remembering a snatch of a gospel song played often on the radio that she liked to sing about angels watching over her.

I was too young really to take part when Aunt Anna Mae died. My last memory of her, though I didn't know at the time she was dying of cancer, was of her sitting in a favorite stuffed chair. Her apartment was in dim light, and she grinned at something youthful and stupid I must have said. When I think of her I remember only that grin. Amid the hustle and confusion and grief of their passing, there was little opportunity to write anything special for Aunt Emma or Aunt Bessie. So I have, instead, put something in words here. I realize that my aunts offered me, collectively, proud examples of self-sufficiency, the joy (and pain) of living, that overworked black woman's trait of strength and resourcefulness.

Aunts Emma, Bessie, and Anna Mae, and my father, never finished high school. So Aunt Rosie was especially proud that she had not only persevered and gained her high school diploma but had also earned her credentials as a licensed practical nurse. When I neared my high school graduation, she was ebullient and was amazed that I planned to travel so far from Philadelphia to the University of Southern California in Los Angeles for undergraduate studies.

When my aunts were young, the family moved to Philadelphia from Statesville, North Carolina. Aunt Emma worked for much of her life in a pickle factory and bought her own building, where she lived, rented apartments, and ran a speakeasy. When I was small, all I knew was that at Aunt Emma's, there was always a party. Aunt Bessie, a faithful member of a Baptist church, lived in her entire house, a wide, three-story row house near Philadelphia's old Connie Mack baseball stadium. A white man rented the front porch/vending area on game nights to sell Phillies memorabilia before the stadium was torn down. The last time I saw her, at the home she had moved to in North Carolina with her third husband, she was so happy to see my sister Elaine and me and happy that we had come to help her clean, make repairs, and maintain her home. That was just a year before she died.

Now I gather what pieces of the past that I can as I adjust to a time when my post–civil rights generation moves into our middle years, adjust to a time of fewer illusions. I thank my aunts and their entire generation of black women for the fortitude that they tried to pass on to us. I thank them for imparting a sense of honesty about how life is lived. I thank them for a strong spine and clear sight. I thank them for showing me about love, love of self, how to love a man when that is the right thing, and how to leave a man when that is the right thing, how to pass on to my young son and future children something that will keep them in the future. So that just as my aunts have been an example to me, I can be an example of something strong and progressive, not weak, passive, or disingenuous.

I'm thankful for this small space to say something about these special women in my life who have passed on, having never been written about by anyone else for any reason. As I fight for my own stories, I feel I fight for both my personal history and our collective history. Intertwined with this fight for voice is respect for our past and therefore some control of our future.

Aunt Emma, Aunt Bessie, Aunt Anna Mae, and Aunt Rosie, I love you.

Keep watching over me.

Of Aunties and Oak Cabinets

PAMELA JOHNSON

When I was sprouting up in southern California in the 1960s and 1970s, the grocery store up the road gave out S&H green stamps to make loyal customers out of folks like my mom. Week after week, she returned to buy more food and collect more stamps. She'd paste them in a special S&H book, while coveting the lamps, radios, and electric can openers displayed tantalizingly in the catalog.

I don't remember us receiving a single thing for all her efforts, and I suspect my recent discovery of forty stamps is unlikely to earn me any prizes. Nonetheless, I was charmed to see them slide from the shelves of an oak cabinet as I moved it from one side of my Harlem apartment to the other a while back. That piece of furniture, and the apartment, belonged to my aunt "Tha."

She was, like me, in her thirties when she moved into the apartment more than three decades ago. Sometimes, as I clean a room or reorder a closet, I am reminded of our vastly different lives. In the kitchen, for instance, she had not one, but two pressure cookers, a Siamese chafing dish (with twin Bunsen burners), a crank-handled forerunner to the Cuisinart, waffle irons, grill units, and enough Tupperware to store leftovers from a White House dinner party. Daddy, Aunt Tha's baby brother, still speaks fondly of meals she made for him. Clearly I'm fruit that fell far from this branch of the family tree, entering the kitchen mostly to spoon jar spaghetti sauce on boiled pasta or steam a salmon steak and some broccoli.

Aunt Tha was a wallpaper woman, while I take my rooms cool and bare. In preparation for having the place painted a couple years back, I scraped and scraped what she had applied strip by strip. She even papered the insides of closets, as well as the tops and insides of the boxes that camouflaged her mini washing machine and deep freeze.

Aunt Tha had skills. She made her own silk dresses and matching coats. They gave her a certain star quality. In her spare time, when she wasn't presiding as a captain at a New York City women's prison, she sewed for whole wedding parties. And she knitted like she had an African village to clothe. My hands know little beyond writing checks for services rendered, jotting the odd note card and tapping computer keys. Just thinking about Aunt Tha's perpetual industriousness makes me want to curl up in a store-bought afghan and take a nap.

My auntie proved virtually tireless. She gleefully traveled the neighborhood and often the world to get in on a good poker game, occasionally pulling an all-nighter. Even in the wee hours, she kept track of each card as it made its appearance. She had decks with her name printed on them. One, in typical Aunt Tha fashion, instructed players to "Make Checks Payable to Thelma Hampton." I, on the other hand, have never been able to keep track of what's trump or who led. I retired from the sport in the early 1980s to silence the groans of college classmates.

Aunt Tha's laser-sharp logic could cut through most matters. But when she'd explain how she'd figured them out, I would respond with a knowing nod, hoping we could move on to the next subject before she smoked me out.

I have to give it to her. In almost all respects, Aunt Tha was ahead of her time. And yet I don't know that she was any luckier in love. She tied the knot three times, and a little slip of paper that I found in a nightstand suggests that the last marriage busted up after only eight months. While I have yet to breeze down the aisle a first time. But I'm in no hurry. For me, once would be quite enough.

I tend to go easier on indulgences, as well. Unlike my auntie, I had the benefit of growing up during the health-aware 1980s and 1990s. I don't smoke, and I exercise regularly. Aunt Tha, on the other hand, came of age in an era when it was fashionable to give them glamour with a wave of your cigarette holder. And she inhaled, early and often. On top of that, she ate heartily from the red meat and dessert food groups, while never moving a muscle unless she had to.

Pamela Johnson

Ultimately, her body swelled to nearly three hundred pounds. Her girth and her premier skill strode hand in hand: with her imposing voice and unimpeachable authority, she could get you to fetch something from any room while she remained seated in her favorite plastic-covered, living room chair. The woman issued orders, then softened them with a girlish, naughty laugh: "Go in the bedroom. Now, in the closet, on the second shelf, to the right of the red box, to the left of the black hat, there is a needle. Tee hee hee hee." And of course, every item she requested would be right where she said it was.

For many years, I viewed this seek-and-ye-shall-find ritual as a reflection of her sheer laziness, as well as her excellent command of others. But near the end, she had to conserve energy. Emphysema shrunk her lung capacity to 30 percent. She drew her life's breath from an apartment-length straw connected to an oxygen tank. Inside her, a hernia twisted angrily. The doctors let it be, wary of complications from cutting through so much fat.

It was in these later, infirm years that Aunt Tha stopped spanning the globe, and I moved to New York City. We grew closer talking about woman stuff, life, sex (she could be bawdy), and personal growth. I loved that we transcended our auntie and niece roles to become girlfriends. Soon, however, our hours together dwindled to none.

Now I am getting to know Aunt Tha through the things she left behind. Foreign currency I find in the folds of a couch add entries to her travelogue; cleaning out a closet full of her furs and sequined hats reminds me of her proclivity to make a grand entrance; and her dozens of pairs of shoes, all given away now, make me chuckle at her eccentricity: She bought nine-and-a-halfs—a half-size larger than she needed—to accommodate her toenails, which she preferred to wear long.

Aunt Tha liked everything just so, which makes me uncertain if she would approve of where I've placed her oak cabinet. Or if she would appreciate the new, paperless walls or the maize color I've painted over the dark rust hues she'd selected. There is so much I will never know.

And then there are the occasional, unexpected discoveries that slip out seemingly from nowhere. Like the S&H green stamps I have been lucky enough to redeem for memories.

Black Swan

SHAWN KENNEDY

What brings me joy when I think about my aunt Mary Lightfoot was her style and flair. I remember Mary amid a kaleidoscope of colors. Hot pink for the silk lounge outfit with gold thread details, inspired by Indian sari cloth that she wore for house parties in the late 1960s.

Green for the chunky rope of beaded sea-glass necklace made from Coke bottles that she discovered in an open-air market while on vacation in Rome. Years before sea-glass jewelry became fashionable, she added it as witty touch to her simple sleeveless shifts.

Gold for the charms that gleamed at her wrists each time she wore my favorite bracelet. It was more than a piece of jewelry; the bracelet was a prompt for wonderful stories of her trips abroad. When she added a tiny gold rickshaw from Hong Kong, I remember Mary recalling with delight her surprise at hearing Chinese schoolchildren speak English with a British accent. The bolero hat charm from Spain would inevitably lead to stories about nightlife in Madrid. And Mary's geta charm, a gold replica of the traditional wooden platform sandal would remind Mary of the public gardens of Kyoto and Tokyo, her favorite places to see Japanese women in traditional dress.

And a certain shade of orange triggers a delicious memory of a giddy 1960s shopping trip with Mary to Chicago's Gold Coast, an area chocked full of trendy boutiques, restaurants, and nightclubs. I wanted a special outfit for my first real date. In boutique after boutique, my ever-elegant aunt tried to steer me toward something chic, but my mind kept skipping back to the sherbet-colored minidress I spied in the first shop we hit. To me that dress was the height of British Carnaby Street cool. I dragged her back one more time to see the dress and try it on. As I twirled before her in a dressing room mirror, she laughed, rolled her eyes, and pulled out her checkbook, saying: "I guess you'll need a pair of white go-go boots with that."

Mary's style was innate, sort of a genetic marker for the women in her family. Mary's mother, my grandmother, was always a smart dresser who wore her pointy-toed pumps into her sixties. Mary's sister, Shirley, my mother, returned from four years in Japan with a wardrobe full of dresses and suits by Parisian designers who opened boutiques in Tokyo while we lived there in the early 1960s.

Although a lifelong resident of the South Side of Chicago, Mary's husband, Louis Lightfoot, was an avid traveler. Together they saw the world, and Mary had beautiful things from every corner of it. From Florence she bought back luscious leather handbags and gloves for the women on her gift list. After a trip to Japan, Mary made a wall hanging of a brocade obi, the sash worn by Japanese women over their kimonos. I still have silver bangles Mary gave me and her other young nieces after her trip to Acapulco.

As the daughter of an air force pilot, I had my own adventures abroad. But while my parents' philosophy was to travel economically and to experience other countries as close as possible to the way natives do, for Mary and Louis it was first class all the way. Mary whetted my appetite for the pleasures of big, beautiful bathrooms in the hotels of Europe and Asia and the luxury of hiring private guides to explore foreign cities rather than traipse about with guidebook in hand.

A walk though the plaza at Rockefeller Center never fails to pinch my heart with a bittersweet memory of Mary during one of her last visits with me. One evening after a day of sightseeing, Mary insisted that we have dinner at the Rainbow Room rather than the midtown bistro I recommended. Mary could not believe that after more than a decade living and working in Manhattan, I had never treated myself to at least a cocktail at the fabulous New York City landmark.

And Mary was so generous. Her friends often commented on her kindness, wit, and vivacious beauty. Mary always had the fattest address book in the family although she kept birthdays and anniversaries mostly in her head. Gift giving was a special pleasure for Mary. She never forgot birthdays, anniversaries, or special occasion of any sort. To celebrate our eighteenth birthday, Mary gave me and my twin sister, Royal, large teardrop-shaped pearls strung on simple gold chains. I cherish that necklace and still wear it.

No matter where she traveled, Mary's striking, unconventional good looks often brought comments from strangers. They'd ask: "What are you?" or more politely, "Where are you from?" not dreaming her reply would be: "I'm Negro, from Chicago, the South Side."

She was tall with a red-brown complexion, deep-set eyes, and a prominent but regal nose. Those same features that defined her beauty as woman made her a rather plain and self-conscious little girl. Mary was a skinny little kid, taller than most of her playmates, with strong features that overpowered her face as a child. But by her teens, Mary had grown into her exotic face and her height. Snapshots in family albums show her transformation from a shy girl to a young woman who delighted in the knowledge that while she would never be cute, she had a sophisticated beauty that demanded a second look. But ever humble, Mary often joked about her skinny legs and her skimpy eyelashes and brows and often blew off the many compliments she received.

Still her looks drew the attention of legendary magazine publisher John H. Johnson when he was starting *Negro Digest* in the late 1940s, before launching *Jet* and then *Ebony* magazine. Mary was among the magazine's first cover girls. The cover photo I remember best was one my grandmother displayed on a bulletin board in her kitchen until the sun faded Mary's fashionable ski outfit from deep winter hues to odd pastel colors.

While posing for *Smart Woman*, another Chicago-based magazine, Mary's path intersected with a young Gordon Parks, who later emerged as a master in photography and film, with such movies as *Shaft* and *The Learning Tree* to his credit. Just before his career took off in the pages of *Life* and *Vogue* magazines, Parks served as the art director and chief photographer for the pioneering magazine. *Smart Woman* was the brain-child of Alone Feaman, who decided after the war the time was right for a national magazine for women of color.

In the January 1947 debut issue, Mrs. Feaman pledged in her editor's note that *Smart Woman* would "point the way to tomorrow's fashions,

Shawn Kennedy

beauty on a budget, a charming personality, better homes, healthy families, successful careers and good entertainment." I had nearly forgotten about her stint modeling for *Smart Woman* until we found the magazines among my grandmother's things. I regret we never got a chance to talk more about her experiences as a pioneering model in the days when the women in Mary's crowd were more often schoolteachers and social workers.

The fashion photographs Gordon Parks took for that magazine are more than fifty years old, but they retain their freshness and originality. Rather than stick to studio shots, Parks posed Mary and the other models against the backdrop of Chicago's architectural landmarks. In one especially glamorous night shot, Mary was posed in the plaza in front of the Wrigley Building, one of Chicago's most magnificent structures. Mary's statuesque figure in a floor-length sequin gown mirrored the height of the magnificent Wrigley tower.

Much later Mary commented on her brief stint as a model: "We weren't paid, of course. The magazine couldn't spend the money. We did it for the fun of being photographed in beautiful clothes we couldn't afford."

As she grew older and lost a son and her husband, I marveled at her strength, resilience, and independence. Mary remained in astoundingly good health until shortly before her death at seventy-seven. She had long helped to care for friends and family members who weren't as strong and mobile as she was. Even at the end of her working day, Mary sometimes did food shopping, ran errands, and served as chauffeur for friends and neighbors.

Inspired by Mary's kindness and generosity as well as her style, I'll always have fun looking at the pictures of her days as a model. But the photo of Mary that I cherish most is not a polished professional print but a family snapshot taken at a summer barbecue. Stretched out on a plastic lawn chair, wearing simple cotton slacks, a shirt, and canvas Keds, Mary, who died in September 2001, is never more beautiful to me.

The Visit

LALITA NORONHA

"It's pointless," my mother said, shaking her head. "You leave for America on Tuesday. Where's the time?" Her voice broke. "We haven't seen you in four years, and you came home for a week?"

"I tried, Ma," I said, "I came here for a conference, remember? I have no more leave."

"She won't recognize you," my mother said. "It's a waste of time."

"Can she talk?" I asked.

"Oh, can she talk?" Ma said, a smile suddenly lighting her eyes. "When could she not? She's a chatterbox."

Grinning, I wrapped my arms around her. "And you're not?" I teased. "Daddy always called you the monkey wallah's drum, remember?" I rolled my tongue against the roof of my mouth, mimicking the sounds my father made. The monkey man had been a part of my childhood. Like the monsoons, he came faithfully every few months, with a pair of young monkeys on his shoulders, a tambourine dangling off his belt, and a makeshift tin drum round his neck. Long before the children of the neighborhood could see him, we heard the drum and flocked into the compound to see his monkey tricks.

"Well," Ma said peevishly, pointing to the ceiling, "your father's sitting up there, and Annie's sitting in the nursing home."

I looked at my mother, a sprightly seventy-four-year-old, wearing the simple cotton dress I'd brought her from the United States. I waited. "Oh, okay, we'll go," she said. "But, she won't know you. It was a bad stroke."

The nursing home, a half hour away by cab, was a dull, rain-washed building flanked by a cluster of coconut trees. The front veranda had several large potted palms and trailing ivy. My mother strode in, sure-footed and familiar with the layout, and smiled at the young receptionist at the front desk. She didn't bother to sign the guest book. I followed her down a short corridor into a big room sprinkled with tables and chairs.

"There! There she is," my mother said, pointing to a crumpled, white-haired woman in a green-print dress. The woman, presumably my aunt, stared blankly at a silhouette of St. Francis, for whom the home, run by the Sisters of Holy Cross, was named. A few half-combed gray heads turned, their grooved faces so crumpled that their eyes seemed to disappear into their sockets, cheeks into chins, mouths chewing cuds of imaginary gum. I stood aside, paralyzed, unable to speak. Suddenly, I had an undeniable urge to run. Take the first flight out of Bombay back to the United States.

"Annie," my mother said, wrapping her arms around my aunt. "It's Mary." She waited. "Your brother Stephen's wife." Something clicked, like a neuronal light switch. "Where is he?" my aunt asked, her beady eyes alert.

"He's dead, Annie. Ten years ago." My mother smiled, pulling up a chair. Impatiently, she gestured for me to come closer. My aunt had been a tall, big-boned woman with a long black braid, a thunderous voice like the monsoons. The last time I saw her she was stirring up a cauldron of mango pickle filled with raisins and dates, the aroma of chilies and vinegar melting under our tongues.

"Auntie," I hugged her awkwardly, "I'm Stephen's daughter. Lalita."

Her face was like warm toast, breath salty. Clasping my hand, she kissed a keloid scar left by our first electric iron.

"Lalita is home from America," my mother explained, proudly. "She came especially to see you."

My aunt's eyes turned to slits. "Why America?" she asked, suspiciously.

"Because she lives there, and has been there for twenty years," my mother answered, deflated.

"Oh! Nobody told me. Nobody tells me anything," my aunt complained.

I leaned forward. "Auntie Annie," I said, "don't you remember? You came to the airport to see me off." Her eyes were blank. My mother shook her head. "Remember, how I had typhoid when I was four years old, and you took me begging? How I almost died!"

Something snapped. "Huh? I took you begging?" she laughed, incredulous. "What nonsense!"

"Yes. You did! You carried me on your hip, like this!" I cried, suddenly betrayed, holding my pocketbook straddled on my waist to demonstrate. Her stories returned with haunting clarity, how she smeared Mercurochrome on her own hand and pretended it was blood, and while I blew on it trying to comfort her, needles jabbed my arm. Then, she held me as I sobbed. "You always trusted me," she would fondly say, years later. "The same Mercurochrome trick, every day," she'd laugh. Sometimes, she'd pinch my cheeks and grin, "Hah, hah, I fooled you." She had loved to tell and retell the story. When I recovered, she said, my mother prayed three rosaries with the spirits one moonless night on the veranda overlooking the church cemetery. Then we went begging door to door in the village for money to feed the poor. That is why I didn't die. And all of it was true because she said so.

My aunt drifted off. "Ma," I said, "you remember her potato *bibique*? You still have her recipe?"

My mother looked at me as if I'd lost my mind. "I make it every Christmas," she said, "but you don't come home." Again, the peevish voice.

"You put coconut milk in it?" I asked.

"Who can make potato *bibique* without coconut milk?" she shot back.

"I want to learn to make it," I said.

"I always want to send you some, but you said no," she said.

"Can't send food to the United States, Ma," I said. "They'll discard it at customs."

"What? My *bibique*?" she cried, her voice two octaves higher.

"*Bibique*?" my aunt said. "You got *bibique*?"

"No, but I brought you cream biscuits," my mother said smoothly, rummaging in her bag, "and Lalita brought you chocolates." I looked at Ma, and she winked. "Two kinds. One plain, one with almonds."

"Shh," my aunt said. "Not here." She stood up abruptly, just as the

Lalita Noronha

bell tolled, calling dinnertime. Feet began shuffling, chairs scraped, everyone stood. And suddenly, there was a clang. A spoon fell off the table, clattering on the tiles. My aunt and I crouched down on our knees averting glares from half-closed eyes. I looked at her hands. Long, brown-knuckled fingers, short nails clipped straight, a yellow gold band worn for more years than I had lived. At least, her fingers hadn't changed.

"Thank you, sweetheart," she said, slipping the spoon in her pocket. "They don't give us eating utensils here, so I hide mine."

I pictured my aunt with a new set of dentures, eyeglasses, and a good hairbrush. Briskly she picked up her walker and took off, my mother and me in tow. Her walker skimmed the floor, as her fingers skimmed along the sand-colored walls like tentacles. Passing the kitchen, then the bathroom, we smelled sizzling fried onions and concentrated urine. Her room, a long, narrow cubicle, had four beds, with adjoining lockers that also served as nightstands. Hers had a glass half full of water, a toothbrush, toothpaste, soap dish, and a vial of tiny white pills labeled "homeopathic medicine for weakness." There was a faint smell of disinfectant and old age. In the twilight, we sat together on the bed; my mother pulled a chair up close.

"And you are . . . who?" She touched my cheek.

"Lalita."

"And who's that?" She pointed to my mother.

"Steve's wife."

There was a moment of oblivion, of pasts, presents, futures churned up in a slurry.

"Give me a ticket to heaven, that's where my Jesus lives," she began to sing, clapping her hands in rhythm.

I clapped, too, while my mother put the biscuits and chocolates on the nightstand. Abruptly, the singing stopped. "No! No. I don't want these. They'll steal them," my aunt cried.

"What? Who'll steal?" My mother turned to me, her eyes suddenly misty.

"But she loves chocolate. I wanted to bring her Swiss Miss!"

She said "Swiss Miss" with a certain pride, like it was something she treasured. I nodded. My mother was referring to instant foods—hot chocolate, oatmeal, "exotic" soups like broccoli and cheese, cream of mushroom, things I often sent her from the States. Sometimes, the packages reached her. Often they were opened and pilfered.

"You can send food packets, and I can't? Not even mango pickle?" she'd often grumbled.

"They're processed foods, Ma," I'd tried to explain, but my mother saw no difference.

"Well, Auntie," I said now, "have a piece of chocolate." I tore open the wrapping and broke off a square. Reaching over, I put a piece in her mouth. She smiled. "Hmm, chocolate," she said. "Who brought chocolate?"

My mother shook her head. "Aiy," she sighed. "We should be going. It's getting late."

As if my aunt had heard, she got up suddenly and walked over to a cupboard she shared with her roommates. Pulling out a dress, the color of cloves, she brought it over to the bed and placed it between us. "This is my other dress," she said. "They wash one; I wear one. No stealing."

"It's pretty," I said.

She looked about furtively. "Pss! I have a secret," she said, thumping her pillow. She smiled impishly, picked up her pillow, and began rocking it side to side, like a doll, humming. Then she put it down carefully, smoothed the folds, and unsnapped the buttons on the pillowcase flap. Inside was a white muslin petticoat with lace around the bodice and hem.

"I'll wear this when I die," she said. "No matter what else I wear, my petticoat is ready. And of course, my veil." Reaching deeper into the pillowcase she unfolded a triangular piece of black lace.

A terrible heaviness, like a dark thundercloud enveloped me. My aunt had raised seven of her own children; "my eighth," she'd called me. "You have two mothers," she'd said. Now she had virtually nothing, not even memory. She had forgotten me and a whole generation of nieces and nephews, decades of family history, wondrous tales of antiquity, dog-eared from telling and retelling, now drowned in waves of opaque and lucid confusion. I watched the contours of her face, each crease, as the salmon light faded into a gray dusk.

"Come, Auntie, it's getting dark," I said, taking her hand. "Let's put everything back."

Lalita Noronha

My mother folded her veil and returned her dress to the cupboard. We left the rest of the chocolates beside the homeopathic pills. "Come tomorrow in the daytime," my aunt said, "so I can see your face."

"You'll come?"

Helplessly, I turned to my mother as she shook her head vigorously. "You leave for America in two days," she whispered, "there's no time."

My aunt signed a cross on my forehead with her thumb, as I bent to kiss her. I tried for the last time. "Auntie," I pleaded. "Auntie Annie. You do know me. Say you know me." She smiled sweetly, and there for the briefest moment our eyes locked. "Give me a ticket to heaven," she said, half singing, waving good-bye.

And now, a year later, my mother's voice over the phone is like a hymn.

"Your aunt died peacefully today," she said. "God is so merciful; she was never really ill, you know." She paused, faltering. "She was older than your dad, but she outlived him by a full ten years—the very last of your grandmother's thirteen children, the end of a generation. You remember how she took you begging. . . ."

I closed my eyes, my mother's voice washing over me like twilight.

Zenda

IMANI POWELL

My aunt Zenda's ass is awesome. God created a perfectly sculpted behind that rounds nearly a foot from the small of her back, accentuating
her tiny waist. It gently sways from left to right as she walks, and
Zenda's ostentatious feature challenges the seams in her size-nine
bubble-gum jeans, which stretch across her hips and cling like a layer
of light blue acrylic paint.

When I was seven years old, her derriere was larger than life. It
blocked my view at times, but overall, it was very pleasant to look at.
I remember walking with Zenda, my little hands wrapped around the
bars of the stroller as she pushed my baby cousin Joey, who sat comfortably, dreaming and sucking on his pacifier. The sun, intensified by the
hot concrete, beat down on us as we made our way to Flushing Mead-
ows Park in Queens. Zenda's honey-blonde highlighted hair rested on
her shoulders in a feathery bob. I remember thinking her small breasts,
flattened from nursing two children, looked like a pair of sunny-side-up
eggs when she was naked. But that day they were held up in a skimpy
stretch tank top.

I watched the men watch her as we passed a group of Dominican
guys pumping merengue in front of the *cuchifritos* and bodegas, and
drinking beer on crowded street corners. Some hissed, others stopped
dead in their tracks. "Goddamn!" they exclaimed. "*Mira ese culo!*" "Look at
that ass!" Others said nothing; instead they undressed her with their
eyes, as if she were a Puerto Rican candy bar. I didn't like it, and I
watched them with contempt, wondering why they couldn't just leave
her alone and let her walk in peace. I looked up at Zenda, but she didn't
seem to mind at all. She didn't even seem to notice. She looked ahead
and continued down the crowded pavement.

But it wasn't always that way. Growing up, Zenda's body slowly blossomed into curvaceousness, much like her mother's, my grandmother Theresa. Hers was the classic bombshell figure, which reminded me of an old-fashioned Coca-Cola bottle. As Grandma Theresa watched her daughter's hips widen, she became concerned and wondered how to protect Zenda. Grandma Theresa eventually became overprotective, making Zenda dress in oversized clothing that downplayed her voluptuousness. She reasoned it was for Zenda's own good. At sixteen, Zenda was prohibited from wearing jeans, dangly earrings, or makeup to school. There were no parties or dates until she was eighteen. And when she finally reached the age of consent, dating consisted of sitting chaperoned, side by side with her first boyfriend, Hector, on the living room couch. Hector would fall asleep, awakening to leave and go visit his other girls—the girls with fewer restrictions. Zenda was married at nineteen to Uncle Robie, a boisterous young man with a large voice and a passion for the Mets, who drove a meat truck.

For the most part, Robie had a good heart. Though looking back, he was threatened by his wife's undeniable appeal. "Men only look at you 'cause of your ass," he would remind her. Back then, part of her believed him; she didn't know any better. At the time, she was too young to see herself and didn't quite understand where her power lay. And her behind seemed like the most likely source. An older, wiser Zenda would say later that he felt a need to diminish her beauty.

One day all that changed when a neighbor called Zenda over to her house. "I need you to go to the store for me," she said. "But first, I'd like you to put on these things. I don't know what your mother is doing to you; you are so beautiful," she said. At first, Zenda protested, then she gave in and slipped into the woman's formfitting clothes and went to the store. The men who sat in the parking lot lost their minds! All eyes were on her. Every head turned. Every man young and old, beers in hand, leaning on their cars, cried out in disbelief: "Wow!" they exclaimed, "Ain't that Mr. Primus's girl?"

Zenda was uneasy. She didn't like the attention that she was getting, particularly not from the same old men who drank in the parking lot with her daddy. Younger men were looking at her hips, her legs, and her behind. She felt exposed and vulnerable. It was a strange feeling. As she rushed back to the project's door, a humble old man about seventy years old, who was also blind in one eye and hobbling down the street with a cane, stopped dead in his tracks. He looked her in the eyes and said, "You are the most beautiful thing I have ever seen."

Something about the way he said it, the way he looked at her, the way he appreciated her beauty, changed things. Maybe I am beautiful, she thought.

Zenda enjoyed the short walk back to her neighbor's house. It was much more than her usual trip through the projects and across the street. For Zenda, it was a turning point. That day she believed that she was beautiful, because that old man had told her so; what reason did he have to lie?

Twenty years later, after a divorce from Robie and two bad relationships, Zenda is in her forties and more confident than ever. She is no longer afraid of her voluptuous beauty, and she won't tolerate anyone who is. She has given up bubble-gum jeans for tailored business suits. Now Zenda shows off her curves in formfitting skirts, her cleavage perfumed and hidden beneath intricate lace that peeks out from her blouse. She wears garters to hold up her stockings. She lengthens her eyelashes with thick black mascara, paints her toenails fuchsia, and slips them into three-inch heels. She adorns each finger with rings of turquoise and precious stones. From her ears, peacock feathers dangle in homage to her femininity. And Zenda doesn't care who is looking as she walks proudly down the street.

I can still remember my mother saying, "I wish she'd put some clothes on; she has no self-respect!" I took note of my mother's comments, but they never really made any sense to me at all because my aunt's energy has always been beautiful and nurturing; she would do anything for anyone. She helped out wherever possible, cooking large pots of yellow rice and gandules, taking in other people's children, consoling us with warm hugs and making orange peel tea for us to drink when we were ill.

My aunt Zenda is now liberated. She is the one who buys all the women in the family lacy thongs for Christmas. She winks at us knowingly as we giggle when we unwrap the delicate lingerie and press them back beneath the tissue paper slightly embarrassed. She is the crazy

Imani Powell

aunt who urges us to learn how to masturbate: "There is absolutely nothing wrong with taking care of yourself," she would say, giggling.

"Oh my goodness." We blushed as she chuckled and enjoyed the shock value of the truth as she saw it. "Well, you shouldn't have to wait for a man; you can take care of yourself, all on your own!" she exhorted us.

Zenda has taught me that a sensual woman is like a powerful river, one that can resist her flow only for so long if she is to survive. A sensual woman, like my aunt Zenda, will find ways to bask in her glory. She'll reflect the sunlight while bringing her wealth, beauty, and power to the world.

Though she is years ahead of me, Zenda has always been close to me. Today we often find ourselves dating at the same time. We would laugh and compare notes; I found joy in the fact that at times her boyfriends were close to me in age. We would school each other, laugh at the downside, experiment with celibacy, invite adventure into our lives; and, throughout it all, she would never forget to remind me: "This is about *you*. This isn't about anyone else, my dear."

Zenda is a relief in a society that doesn't like to talk about sex, yet thrives on exploiting women's sensuality. Men are often threatened by sexually powerful women, women who dare to define themselves in a world that is quick to label them. Zenda refused to allow that to happen to me. Instead she urged me to define and, more important, to find myself. She has encouraged me to be free to find that comfortable place, and if no one else agreed, it was still okay. She accepts me and supports me, and she will be there to laugh or cry with me until I finally get self-respect, self-esteem, and self-celebration right.

Zenda is living proof that the closer you get to that goal, the less afraid you become of tapping into the complete power of unadulterated feminine energy: "I don't care what people say," Zenda says, "I live *for me!*"

Avenging Angels

Hanging On

JIM CIHLAR

Aunt Dolores, I know if you were ever
faced with doubts, you still woke up

an hour early to pack sack lunches.
You were constant as the night-light in your hall,

a beneficent moon. You were scrawny and tough
like the cotton plant in sand in your basement,

which dared to flower because the odds were against it.
You were a rag, a bone, and a hank of hair

as you spooned mashed potatoes and yams and Jell-O
onto your children's plates. I wish I could be like you,

joking your way through loud family reunions
and country-western songs on the record player,

through evenings watching television in the dark,
through all-night poker games, your husband's friends,

beer and cigarette smoke. Aunt Dolores, you've known
all along we all must be deserted sometime,

the way cotton seeds fall away from the stem,
and that is why you sent your kids to school

every morning with a kiss and a shove,
pushing them away from you.

Jim Cihlar

Dancing Behind the Glass

MARILYN BATES

Aunt Lilly sat resolutely in the rocking chair on our front porch on Market Street with an old-fashioned blackjack hidden in the folds of her apron. The blackjack she held wasn't the slick metal bar sheathed in leather that was used in 1940s gangster movies. It was brown-rubber ugly, with hairs arrayed like a golf ball suddenly let loose. Fritz Coleman, its intended victim, swaggered confidently down the street toward our house. He had come to face my mother, who accused his wife of consorting with my father on those nights he pretended to wash the venetian blinds at the Fort Steuben Hotel. More like a character in a stage play than a defender of his wife's name, Fritz was almost comic in his loud yellow salesman's jacket, the one he wore in the cattle yards to hawk meat at two pennies a pound.

A German immigrant, Fritz had made his way in the world as a meat trader, and he owned a wholesale butcher shop. On Sundays he promenaded down Fourth Street tipping his hat, feigning the cultured manners of a gentleman. But we laughed at him because he was unsophisticated, his jackets always garish, and the soles of his shoes worn down at the outer edges so that his feet splayed as he sauntered down the street with his wife, Mabel, on his arm.

My mother had called Fritz, sobbing uncontrollably on the phone as she told him of his wife's betrayal. But he reacted by denying it and swore to make Mother swallow her words. Outraged by my mother's call, he told her he was not going to take the word of a simpering Guinea woman who had accused his wife of cavorting with her husband. Everyone in town knew that Fritz was an old cheater who harassed the women who worked for him, especially the pretty young ones he kept after closing to mop floors, clean counters, and tend books.

If it hadn't been that his wife was cheating on him with my father, we would have felt he got his just deserts.

Now he stood at the foot of our front steps, facing Lilly primly seated in her best attire. Her real name was Pasqua, which means Easter in Italian, but we called her Lilly like the flower because it was easier to pronounce. On that particular day she took on a new role, not just as our aunt but also as our protector, a role she assumed after Uncle Frank and my grandfather died, leaving us with no men in our family, except my father, who was always out working two jobs.

Fritz's visit was almost as painful as the day my mother took me to the Hub Department Store to confront Mabel Coleman at the very place where she and my father worked. Mabel, her blonde hair wrapped in a smooth twist, remained calm and aloof through the ordeal. She reminded me of those posters of World War II pinup queen Betty Grable smiling smugly over her shoulder at the G.I.s who patted her behind as they parachuted out of planes.

Mother came unglued. Her words gushed out as Mabel stared down disdainfully, unmoved by her trembling voice. I didn't understand all of the words, but I knew that Mother was in trouble. Mabel picked up the phone to call my father, who managed the second floor. But it was too much to face them together, and my mother was afraid that the look on their faces would confirm that the stories her friends told her were true. So we fled down the fire escape, like angels cast out of heaven, too embarrassed by my mother's sobbing to take the elevator.

Now Fritz had come to our house to make my mother take back her lies and accusations. I stood frozen inside the house, hiding behind the crystal facets of our glass front door, opened just a crack so I could hear. Fritz undoubtedly had a few drinks to bolster his courage, for his face was tinged by a pink mask, and sweat stained the armholes of his jacket. As he stumbled up the steps, Lilly showed no emotion or fear. Lilly began rocking back and forth in her chair until the moment he reached the top step. Then suddenly, as if choreographed in advance, she rose and gracefully raised her hand above her head, the blackjack clenched in midair, her step perfectly timed to match his approaching gait. "You take-a one more step, and I'm gonna bumble your brains," she said in broken English.

Marilyn Bates

175

Fritz stopped. He made no move and stood there on the porch staring at Aunt Lilly, who was a formidable woman. She was as tall as he, a matronly figure with large sagging breasts and strong arms that plumped her sleeves. Maybe Fritz was afraid of this woman poised there so defiantly, or afraid of losing his dignity. This was the 1940s, and a man would never strike a woman unless he was a rogue. And Fritz was no rogue; after all, he had come to defend his wife's name. I watched his face—a jigsaw of patterns through the glass. I saw his lips move as he said something to Lilly, his voice an unintelligible garble. He shifted his hat into his other hand, animatedly pointing his finger toward his chest as if speaking about himself. Lilly, arm still raised, said not a word. As he paused at the threshold, something must have crossed his mind. Slowly, he put his hat on his head, backed one foot down on the pavement, followed by the other. Lilly lowered her arm as Fritz turned and walked away down Fourth Street.

Years later, I would look at a picture of Lilly and remember a woman gray beyond her years, with a scowl on her face, and her hair in wispy disarray. It was almost as if she were humoring the picture taker, perturbed at being called away from the washboard where she scrubbed Uncle Frank's soot-ridden work clothes. I would wonder when I looked at that picture whether all the married women who came from the old country let themselves age, go gray, and surrender their youth to marriage. Perhaps they took on this look of dowdiness to share in the eternal sadness of their husbands who left the cool mountains of Italy for America, where they pounded spikes in railroad ties burnished with their sweat.

As the oldest of six children, Lilly had left home first when she married Uncle Frank, a male nurse. They moved to Rome where Frank worked in a clinic, and they went to all the operas. When they immigrated to the United States, Lilly and her sister, my grandmother, would often sing songs from the Italian operas, especially during canning season on a Sunday afternoon when they listened to Verdi, Rossini, or Puccini on the radio. They loved *La Traviata* best and would sing to each other, pantomiming the words of lovers and bursting into laughter, their rising voices mocking the tragic moments.

Their raucous merriment was perhaps a momentary escape from reality, their disappointments. They lived in a small mill town, where Uncle Frank had to choose between work as an orderly at the local hospital or a union job with better pay but brutal labor that broke his spirit. His smooth, sensitive hands that once kneaded obstinate muscles or debrided wounds into healing were coarsened by calluses and dirty fingernails that only harsh soap and a stiff brush could remove.

Whatever his motive for Fritz's retreat that day, we never mentioned the incident again. We went on as we always did—after my father's obsessive drinking when the story unraveled, after he ran off with Mabel, leaving the new inventory at the Hub Department Store for the owners to figure out, and later after Uncle Frank's untimely death from prostate cancer. We bought clothes on the time-payment plan, stared the butcher in the eye over an ounce of fat, traded life insurance policies for tuition, and mended our own broken hearts.

The evening after Fritz left, we went on with our household chores. Assembled in the kitchen my mother washed chickpeas, my grandmother pummeled dough into pliant loaves, and at the stove Lilly stirred basil into a dimpled kettle of fresh tomatoes popping their skins in the boiling water.

Marilyn Bates

Blood Sense

MARK HOLT-SHANNON

As kids, my brothers and I often took the Greyhound north from San Diego, California, to visit Aunt Lolly in Oxnard. Traveling without an adult felt a little scary, but the risk was outweighed by our shared sense of urgency to see the Listons—our three cousins, Uncle Tom, and the ringleader, Aunt Lolly. Something happened when we were all together again—fishing, swimming, listening to George Carlin records, screaming in the dark as Uncle Tom once again told us the story of the man with the golden arm, or watching home movies. I especially loved those movies. I can still hear the clicking of the projector, the blowing of the fan, the laughter as we pointed at moving pictures of ourselves. Suddenly, my real dad would show up on screen, so young and responsible and funny. He'd make faces, scare me or my brothers, and imitate our clumsy toddler walk. Watching him, we'd laugh, though not as loudly, not as easily. Aunt Lolly would narrate the silent movies, rattling off the names and relationships and brief histories of the people on screen I'd never met but who looked vaguely, longingly familiar. I'd cling to her during those moments, and even though she held me too tight sometimes, I never seemed to mind.

The bus ride always seemed so much farther north than I ever remembered from the previous trip. But once we cleared the smog and turbulent traffic, and reached the altitude just above Los Angeles, we searched for two markers. First, the stout, flat-topped citrus trees. Since orchard after orchard of those perfectly arranged rows seemed all that stood between me and another Aunt Lolly bear hug, I imagined them first as speeding torpedoes whose blows I absorbed with gritted teeth, then as a string of Pac-Man power dots that I devoured open-mouthed as we sped northwest.

Mostly, though, I just pressed my head against the window, angled my gaze to manipulate the rate at which the rows scrolled by. In this way, they seemed to elapse as I counted them, every sixty seconds, another minute, another mile.

The real marker that my brothers and I still remember and reminisce about was a single row of gigantic eucalyptus trees. I always began searching for them too soon, opening myself up each time to the creeping feeling of change or lost magic. "Are they gone?" I'd wonder. "Did I only imagine them?"

It was as if this family of trees was the Listons themselves, who I feared losing ever since my mom and dad divorced. I'd eventually spot the trees to the northeast, towering and shimmering in the overcast distance. "Is that them?" I'd ask, tapping my finger on the glass.

"Are those the trees?" We would huddle nose-close as the trees came into view. "Yep," Tommy, my oldest brother, would finally confirm nonchalantly, as if the storm raging in my stomach wasn't also raging in his. "That's them. Almost there."

My aunt's real name was Eleanor, though Uncle Tom was the only person I ever heard call her that. To everyone else she was Lolly, Aunt Lolly, or Lol. Hearing my mom call her Lolly when I was a child, I sensed their familiarity and understood that despite the fact that Mom had divorced Aunt Lolly's brother and remarried, our relationship with the Listons would endure.

Aunt Lolly had three brothers: Uncle Patrick, a New Jersey police officer I've met once or twice; Uncle Danny, a New York police officer I've never met; and my dad, a retired butcher who I believe lives in Arizona. I used to rationalize having family I've never met—a reunion's worth of uncles, aunts, tiered cousins, half brothers, and half sisters—by transforming them into gifts I would open later in my life. Moving east nearly fifteen years ago should have been the perfect opportunity to open these gifts. But I hesitated, dreamily waiting for Aunt Lolly to organize an East Coast reunion where we'd all come together in some backyard, shake our heads over how much we've grown, and drink ourselves into conversation.

Mark Holt-Shannon

We always boarded the bus early in San Diego. Mom would come on with us, letting the driver know that we were her three boys by touching our heads. She'd take one of our tickets and wave it in the driver's face to let him know that we were going to Oxnard. "To see their aunt Lolly," she'd say, smiling. She sat us near the front, in three of the four seats making up an entire row on both sides of the aisle. Sometimes that fourth seat remained empty, though mostly it did not. I would volunteer to sit alone because it was the surest way to get a window seat, and sitting with strangers was never as bad as I expected. If I wanted to be left alone, I'd stare out my window. But when the conversation did come, it was usually fine, one-way chitchat, like answering easy test questions or filling out biographical paperwork that doesn't require consulting your mother. Where are you from? How old are you? What subjects do you like? Do you have a girlfriend? (Smile.) Who do you know in Oxnard? Your aunt Lolly? Is she your mother's sister or your father's?

I remember the strangers who plopped down next to me as kind, curious elderly ladies mostly, who wore hats, kept packages in their laps, and offered mints. My stoicism eventually softened, and soon I was initiating conversation about my cousins—Tom, Matt, and Delia— and how they were the same ages as me and my brothers, about Uncle Tom, a big Irishman who worked as a sheriff at a prison workfarm, where they raised chickens and slaughtered pigs. "He even takes us there," I'd say. I also talked about Aunt Lolly, my real dad's sister, a nurse and a crazy woman who always does something loud and funny when we get there. "You might even see," I'd tell them.

And whatever magnificent scene Aunt Lolly orchestrated—horns, whistles, skits, impressions, and signs—it was typically loud. When my brothers and I come together at Christmas, we still shake our heads and reminisce, "Remember the pots and pans?" I nod. But what I remember most vividly is how when Aunt Lolly laughed, which was often, she'd collapse in on herself, often reaching out for a shoulder to steady her.

I don't know my real dad well, and my memories of him have become fuzzy, as if I've traveled out of memory's range and could one day soon completely lose reception. One memory that does stand out in my mind is the day, with Chris and me in tow, he swaggered into a high-class steak house wearing cowboy boots, dungarees, and a buttoned-down shirt with the sleeves rolled up. I was fifteen, Chris thirteen; Tommy was overseas. "Yeah, sweety," he said to the cute young waitress standing over us, pen and pad poised, "Can I get a grilled cheese sandwich and a cherry Coke." (I still use that joke in fancy restaurants.) I laughed because that's not what he wanted. I laughed at his unwavering delivery. I laughed at how our waitress hesitated, smiled, and spun completely around: "You guys." And I felt grateful. We hadn't seen him in years, and he helped us through by lightening things up. I guess we helped him by laughing.

Though I can't recall a time when they were together in my presence, Aunt Lolly and my dad were clearly related. Like him, Aunt Lolly was tall, with a handsome, yet hard and slightly drawn face. But the feature that connects them the most is their enduring, idiosyncratic sense of humor. In fact, my wife says that living with me, being a part of my family, is like being trapped in an episode of *The Three Stooges*. It is a burlesque, slapstick life of feigned collisions with stationary objects, mockery, and self-debasement, and of pointing out imaginary irregularities on each other's person as a setup for the finger-up-the-nose gag.

When visits with my real father sputtered and then stopped, yearly and sometimes twice-yearly visits to Aunt Lolly did not. But even in the heartiest of those visits, no matter how our temples ached or our eyes teared from laughter, we were bound to slam into a mention of my dad. We abruptly fell from our euphoric reunion into an awkward silence. Aunt Lolly hovered around us in those moments, doling out soda and paper plates heavy with chips and sandwiches. She never apologized for my real dad, never bad-mouthed him, but simply restarted our engines.

"Marky, lean over, sweety," Aunt Lolly would say. "You get chips on my floor, and I'll ring your little San Diego neck, you hear me? Oh, my gosh, Marky, what is that coming out of your nose? Is that boogers? It's mustard; here's a napkin, love." She'd open the napkin, palm the top of my head with one hand, and roughly wipe my entire face, ears and all, with the other. "Thank God, I thought we was going to have to take you to the emergency room for yellow boogers. Who needs a sandwich? Who needs soda? Give me a bite of that, you little hog. And some of your soda. Oh! That's good."

She'd kiss us all on our heads and then whack us in the same spot.

Mark Holt-Shannon

She'd sit in my chair, scooching me onto the carpet, while my brothers and cousins fell to the floor holding their stomachs. She'd bring my sandwich to her open mouth and then, suddenly, pretend to notice me. "What are you doing on the floor, Marky?"

It was in her joking and her honesty about the fact that my father had split that I knew how strong I could be. Even the way she joked as if I didn't matter showed me how much I did.

As the bus lurched and wound toward Oxnard, and my stomach whirled like a cotton candy machine, I felt warmed by the smiling eyes of my travel companion. I'd feel the eyes of other travelers in nearby seats who, charmed, turned to listen to our conversation. I'd even catch the driver smiling back at me, his face vibrating in the gigantic rearview mirror. I imagined that as the bus turned and bounced into the station, these people searched excitedly out their own windows, hoping to catch a glimpse of our cousins, Uncle Tom, and the magical aunt Lolly.

"The Shannons are here!" I'd hear Aunt Lolly shout as our feet hit the pavement. Embarrassed, our cousins sometimes hid behind her, covered their eyes, or might even stand next to some other family. That was not Aunt Lolly's concern. As Uncle Tom collected our luggage, I stood inside Aunt Lolly's arms, beaming, inadvertently catching a stranger's eye: "See! Did I tell you?" Sometimes these strangers, with their coats on and their bags underarm, would shuffle reverently toward Aunt Lolly and lay a hand on her as if she were Our Lady of Medjugorje. They'd speak words I could not hear from below but I knew were kind. Aunt Lolly, always gracious, would return the touch, maybe even a hug.

She was the one who tacked the affectionate Y's onto our names. Even the very last time I saw her, she called me her little Marky, called my brothers Tommy and Chrissy, and Mom, Pammy, as if the Y protected and insulated us from indifference. "Oh, my sweet, precious Marky boy," she said then, grabbing my hands. "Oh, you're soaking wet. It's okay, love, don't worry about your aunt Lolly; when I'm better, you'll see." Then she said something I have always felt: "Oh, what is it, my Marky? What is it about you?"

Maybe there's a hole in someone abandoned. If I had one, she helped fill it, as did others: my mom and the godsend of a man she married later, my stepfather, the man whom I would call father. "When your dad walked out on youze guys," Uncle Tom told me with his thick, nail-pounding, gin-and-stout-drinking, cigar-smoking, loving Irish hands on my shoulders, "he walked out on all of us." It had never occurred to me that my brothers and I weren't my father's only victims: when he turned away from us, he turned away from his sister, too.

I feel I've forgiven my father for his madness. And though I do not feel I've suffered from it, I do think about him and his absence a great deal, about how I will feel when he dies. My brother Chris it seems was young enough just to forget. "It's cool," he'd say. And Tommy was old enough to banish with a "Fuck him." Maybe being in the middle left me with a particularly gaping hole, and my struggle to fill it was more apparent, which Aunt Lolly detected.

I remember visiting her as a young man, drifting toward her in the kitchen, the two of us alone. While she leisurely washed each dish, I leaned back against the counter and could see my father in her silhouette. She nodded, cautiously answering questions about his whereabouts. She was my informant, my link, but to more than just my real father.

I don't long for a relationship with my father. What I long for, what I needed and got from Aunt Lolly, was a genetic link, a sense of heritage and history and some blood sense.

The reunion I'd waited for finally occurred, and though Aunt Lolly was instrumental in its planning, she never made one phone call, never sent one invitation. It would have been the perfect—well, maybe not perfect—opportunity to meet many of my still unopened gifts. But I couldn't afford to make the trip. Eleanor Liston died from cancer not two weeks after I last saw her. She is the first person of profound significance in my life whom I have lost. Thankfully, that warm California winter afternoon in her den I was able to lay my head on her chest and say good-bye. What I never said was that I'm sorry your brother turned out to be incapable of having a relationship with you, me, any of us, and that I'm okay. The hole is just about filled.

I'm a Shannon, Aunt Lolly. I'm a Shannon and, thanks to you, I am proud of that. Oh, and Aunt Lol, one more thing—you got a little something there on your blouse.

Mark Holt-Shannon

183

The Warden

MICHELLE PINKARD

"Hello, Aunt Corrine, is that you?"

Her voice was raspy and frail, a startling contrast to the choppy commands that used to cut through Winston menthol cigarette smoke all the years I had known her.

"Yes, baby, it's me," she hacked. "I have a little cold I can't shake. How are you doing? It's good to hear from you."

The hint of a smile in her voice was encouraging, but this would still be hard. I hadn't seen or spoken to Aunt Corrine in over three years, but somehow she was always on my mind. Hidden beneath all my ambitions, goals, and desires was the hope that I would somehow, someday make her proud.

For a woman of her gifts and demands, that would not be easy. Her tongue was a sassy and quick whip—impressive to watch, but it could sting at a whim. Knowledge was her power, and the few who challenged her cursed the fact that they had to live to regret that decision.

We muddled through niceties. I asked about her consulting business; she asked about the man in my life, or lack thereof.

"Well, Aunt Corrine, I am sure you are wondering why I called. I will get straight to the point." My heart thudded. "I know it's been a long time since we talked. And I apologize for that. Things have been crazy here.

"But as I look at my life, the course it's taking and where it's going, my blessings and the lessons I am learning from my failures, I realized a call was long overdue. I realized I gave you a hard time all those years we stayed with you."

She laughed. "Oh honey, you were angry. You had a lot to be angry about, and that was a long time ago."

"I know, Aunt Corrine, but I was just calling to give you an overdue thank-you. I was thinking back to that time we read a collection of poetry together, I forget the title, but we were reading it and you said something that has never left me."

I could feel her listening as I continued. "You said that one day, you would see my name in one of those collections. It struck me because I never even had that thought. In retrospect, I realize that was the day I learned to dream."

Aunt Corrine had this presence, this innate power that is instilled in black women from birth but that usually takes another black woman to unleash. My grandmother and her gun-toting sisters had tapped into Aunt Corrine's power. I met her long before I had discovered mine.

Some ten years ago, months before my sixteenth birthday, Momma decided to take me and my younger brother to live with her sister as a last resort. Drugs, crime, and a part-time father had already failed to save our crumbling family. After hours on the road, the three of us arrived homeless, hapless, and hungry on Aunt Corrine's doorstep in Corpus Christi, Texas.

She greeted us with a smile and a cigarette. She was a short, round woman who barely pushed five-two even wearing three-inch heels. Her curly black hair tapped her shoulder with every movement. Smooth, chocolate brown skin made it impossible to guess her age. . . . Was she forty-four, forty-three . . . forty?

As my brother and I rushed to unload our belongings from the car, Ma and Aunt Corrine embraced so hard and so long it seemed as if time itself stopped. In that moment, life made sense. The thirty-five-hour trek from Omaha, Nebraska, to Corpus Christi, leaving behind the chaotic life we knew made sense. But our comfort was short-lived.

My brother and I would soon learn the harsh realities of southern child rearing. The lessons would come quick. Our failure to conform had a ripple effect, stinging sharper than any leather belt. We received a condescending lecture, and worse, we shamed our mother. Her punishment was the worst insult of all, she felt the shame of being labeled a bad mother.

The underlying theme of all Aunt Corrine's lessons was simple enough. Children were children, adults were adults; there would be no

Michelle Pinkard

confusion or integration. Children were to speak one way, adults another. When adults spoke, children listened. Children spoke when adults permitted. Adults were to be revered, children were to be disciplined. For two northern kids, forced to become self-sufficient as Momma worked several jobs to pay bills, we felt trapped in some warped reality. We were gagged, choked, and beaten by an outdated system, and its enforcer was a bitter woman who didn't understand, couldn't understand the life we came from.

She dared to insist on "Yes, ma'am" when a simple "What?" would do. She demanded that I wear dresses and ribbons when my baggy jeans and baseball caps were comfortable enough. Aunt Corrine forbid us to watch R-rated movies when we had seen more death on the streets than anything Hollywood could produce. There were no *Def Comedy Jam* jokes about humping and masturbation. We already knew enough to educate our sex-ed teachers.

"I'm trying to teach you something," she'd repeat. "I am trying to teach you something."

"What is it; just say it already," we would snap back.

"You will understand one day."

We'd roll our eyes to the corners of our head (behind her back, of course), and life would continue with new restrictions and sanctions for two unruly kids. Our pleas to Momma were understood, but worthless. She could do nothing but succumb to Aunt Corrine's power. My aunt had the money, the house, and the food. Momma kept quiet over basic necessities.

Soon, two male cousins moved into Aunt Corrine's homemade penitentiary. We were all at the warden's mercy.

At some point, Aunt Corrine became creative with her control. The house, she declared, would now run like a business. School was our full-time job, our pay was in accordance with our performance. Our payday was report card day. A's were $20, B's were $10. With seven classes and four semesters, there was some serious money to be made by teens with no obligations and no other means of income.

It was no mystery how four struggling kids who flirted with dropping out grudgingly became college-bound honor-roll students. Teachers didn't understand how the quiet new kids in the room had edged to the front of the class and begged for extra-credit work. Our teachers coped with being harassed over grades and negotiating with determined teenagers come report card time.

Our paycheck did not cover the rent, however. We paid our cost of living with household chores that rotated weekly among the four of us: yard detail, bathroom maintenance, kitchen and dining duty, and cuisine captain.

Worksheets were created for every chore, and on Sunday, or crossover day, the list and inspection were scrutinized. The worker stuck with kitchen duty, for example, would have to check off the items he completed daily:

Wash and dried dishes, check.

Cleaned microwave, check.

Took out garbage, check.

Mopped floor, check.

Check.

Check.

Check.

Check.

There were lists for other chores. The cuisine captain had to plan the meals for the week, shop for items necessary to prepare the meals, and cook for the entire family. Once the daily worksheets were completed, we signed and returned them to the warden. If the warden discovered anything checked that was not completed, the violator was fined at least $1 of his earnings. As hard as it was to earn our money, it was that easy to lose it to a violation.

At the end of a workday, we would huddle.

"The warden has lost her mind," one would say.

"She is never grateful—just work, work, work. Always pointing out what we do wrong."

"Yeah, she has too much time on her hands," another would offer.

"Man, we ain't nothing but slaves here. I am better than this; one day I am going to leave here and show her that I ain't nobody's damn slave!" a younger would proclaim.

"Me too, I just wish she would hurry up and get a man and get some so she could get off our back!"

We would all laugh, and grow stronger leaning on one another.

Perhaps that was her plan, I thought, mulling it over during the silence in our phone conversation. What is she thinking. Knowing her, she was likely forming her well-articulated, well-crafted "I told you so."

"Well, honey, you don't owe me anything. You guys were a gift. You raised yourselves, really. You already had all you needed in you to succeed. And look at you now.

"I am just proud of you."

After Hatred Comes Understanding

YASMIN SHIRAZ

I was twelve years old when I first realized how my aunt Niecey really felt about me. At family reunions, my aunt was friendly with all of my other cousins. But with me, I got a short, curt, "How ya doin'?" in her North Carolina southern drawl. She hugged my other cousins, smiled at them, pinched their cheeks and shoulders. But, with me, it was simply, "How ya doin'?," without so much as a smile or a friendly wave.

As it was, my family was living "up north" in Delaware, and most of my mother's relatives were still living in her hometown of Rocky Mount, North Carolina, the distance already putting space between us. In my short visits, I always tried to get along with my cousins, and become familiar with the rest of my family.

My inquisitive, impressionable preteen mind wondered why my aunt didn't display any loving affection toward me. In fact, I remember telling my mother, "I don't think Aunt Niecey likes me. She's nice to everybody but me." My mother brushed it off and expected me to do so as well. But, I never did. At each family reunion, funeral, family gathering, and holiday, I looked for my aunt Niecey to treat me warmly. And she didn't. Years passed by, and as a young adult, I became flippant toward my aunt Niecey, as I perceived she had been toward me.

When I was about twenty, Aunt Niecey suffered a stroke. She survived but had to stop working. My mother began visiting her in North Carolina twice a month. She bought loungewear and all sorts of intimate items to make her sister feel loved. I couldn't understand why my mom was going out of her way for someone who was so mean to her only daughter. For a while, I attempted to be friendly to her, but as always, she was cool toward me. So, I got over my mean aunt and realized that God had blessed me with seven other aunts.

After graduating from college, I relocated to Upper Marlboro, Maryland, with my mother and brother. I soon got married, and a year later, I had a child, started a business, and began traveling across the country marketing and promoting college-entertainment issues. I would look into the face of my infant and not want to leave her, but I didn't know what else I could do. I needed someone to travel with me, but I couldn't afford to pay a full-time nanny.

Ever resourceful, I called my mom and began to brainstorm ideas with her. In the middle of our conversation, she suggested that I ask Aunt Niecey to travel with me and to watch my daughter while I was attending meetings and conferences. My heart hit the floor. I couldn't dare ask the most evil aunt in the universe to watch my child while I was working. What was my mother thinking to even suggest it? I asked myself. The conversation with my mother ended abruptly, and I ran upstairs to tell my husband the unsavory advice that I had just received. Of course, he didn't think it was a bad idea and reminded me that we didn't have many options.

There had to be another way. I took out my legal pads and jotted down ideas. I searched the Internet for nanny services. I called my babysitter and picked her brain. It was true. We absolutely had no other options. With a heavy heart and my hand on the Bible, I dialed my aunt's phone number. To my surprise, she told me that she would watch my daughter while I was at the conference. A week later, I picked her up in Rocky Mount and we began our first journey.

It was a five-hour trip from Virginia, where I lived, to New Jersey, where the marketing conference was being held. My daughter, barely two months old, sat in the back with Aunt Niecey. I stared at the road, trying to push away negative thoughts. There was an eerie silence in the car when my daughter was asleep. I remembered those family reunions when my aunt wouldn't meet my eyes and when it seemed as if her eyes rolled at the sight of me.

But after a while, we began to discuss politics, her favorite books, and my job. It was easy to break our twelve-year silence once we got started. By the time we arrived in New Jersey, my aunt confided that she was wearing a smoking patch because she didn't want to smoke around my daughter. After that, I made a commitment to forget about our past relationship. The three days at the conference were a blast. I would return to the hotel room in the evenings energized, my daughter and Aunt Niecey excited to see me. Aunt Niecey would tell me about what they had done during the day, and I would tell them all of my marketing ideas. I was so grateful to have my daughter with me, and I knew it wouldn't have been possible without my aunt.

Soon after, my aunt was traveling with me about once a month. I took her to places that she had never been before, and she made me feel like a confident and loving parent because even though I was working, I had my child with me. On a trip to Miami, my aunt marveled at being on a plane for the first time in her life, visiting a place that was so beautiful. She was so happy to be doing something different.

After one of my conference days, Aunt Niecey and I stayed up late talking about family history. She was the family historian, and I never knew it. She knew things about my grandfather and my great-grandfather. She told me about their business ventures and explained that I probably received some of my entrepreneurial spirit from them.

She also shared some of the pain from her childhood with me. Growing up, she felt as if she shouldn't ask for things because her mother couldn't afford much. As a woman in her fifties, her voice still cracked when talking about the things that she wanted to experience but never had the opportunity. Listening to her, I couldn't imagine what it was like. I didn't understand how my aunt was told not to bother filling out college applications because she should focus on helping her mother support the family. I couldn't imagine the pain that she felt, but I was beginning to understand her a little more. Just like that, on the plane from Miami, the reasons for her resentment toward me crystallized in my mind.

I grew up in a nice middle-class suburban neighborhood and never had to share a single thing with my only brother. My parents spoiled us with nice clothes, music lessons, trips to Disneyland, and summer camps. When it was time for me to attend college, the question was not

Yasmin Shiraz

191

if I would go, but simply, where would I be going. When my aunt looked at me, she saw her dreams that were never fulfilled. She saw a selfish child who never had to share with fifteen other siblings. She saw my fine clothes and heard my proper English and assumed I was a young snob.

In my other cousins, she saw little people who shared her experience, and so it was easier for her to show them her love. But there were positive aspects of my upbringing that she couldn't see—the good values, love of family, and integrity that my parents instilled in me. I didn't believe in snobbery. I would never let down a relative.

My appreciation for all that my aunt had been through eroded the ill feelings that I had toward her. Instead of focusing on the love that she withheld from me, I showed her that she would be proud of what I had become—a responsible, cultured, family-oriented young woman.

Those months that we traveled together brought us closer together. My daughter has the relationship with Aunt Niecey that I never had. My aunt, who was never able to have children, now gives me advice about life's issues. I respect her and her opinions.

One recent Mother's Day, I bought her a card that was specially suited for aunts who often fill the role as mother. In my heart, I knew that our relationship had cleared a great hurdle. When I gave her the card, she smiled at me and said, "I like gifts," and chuckled. It's an image that will stay in my mind.

Today, I call my aunt regularly to see how she's doing. When I visit her in North Carolina, I play spades with her, and, on my good days, I beat her handily. I have to remind her that I haven't forgotten where I came from. We laugh, tell stories, and give each other looks of mutual understanding and respect. I never thought my relationship with Aunt Niecey would get to this point, but it has. The hatred is gone, the resentment is gone, the history is there, and the future is still ahead of us.

Wally Amos's Oatmeal Raisin Cookies

(Inspired by Aunt Della. This recipe appeared in Family Circle *magazine.)*

Preheat oven to 375 degrees.

Blend together, and cream:

> 1 cup margarine (2 sticks)
> ¾ cup granulated white sugar
> ¾ cup light brown sugar
> 2 eggs
> 1 teaspoon pure vanilla extract

When thoroughly creamed, sift together and add:

> 2¼ cups all-purpose flour
> 1 teaspoon baking soda
> ½ teaspoon salt
> 1 teaspoon cinnamon

Blend thoroughly, then add:

> 2 cups oats
> 1 cup raisins

When thoroughly blended, drop by teaspoonful onto cookie sheet.
Bake at 375 degrees for 8 to 10 minutes.

Wally Amos

Contributors

BARBARA ADAMS
Last of the Line
Barbara Adams's work has appeared in such magazines and literary journals as *Negative Capability*, *The Nation*, *The Texas Review*, *The Humanist*, and *Full Circle*. She is a member of Poets & Writers, PEN, PSA, and several poetry groups near her upstate New York home. The former Pace University English professor has written short stories, poems, essays, a book of poetry, and a book on Laura Riding. She has also written a play on Sylvia Plath and Ted Hughes that was produced by the Mohonk Mountain Stage Company in New Paltz, New York.

AMINA
The Businesswoman
Amina is an established private chef who incorporates her passion for the culinary arts into her literary adventures.

RAQUELLE AZRAN
Subtle Choices
Raquelle Azran, a native New Yorker, has been living the expatriate life since the late 1960s. She divides her time between Hanoi, Vietnam, where she specializes in Vietnamese contemporary fine art (www.artnet.com/razran.html) and Tel Aviv, Israel, where she writes and edits in her inner-city aerie overlooking the Mediterranean.

MARILYN BATES

Dancing Behind the Glass

Marilyn Bates, author of *It Could Drive You Crazy*, a collection of poetry, is a Poet in Person with the International Poetry Forum and a teacher-consultant at the University of Pittsburgh. Her essays have appeared in *Carnegie Mellon Magazine, Under the Sun, The Pittsburgh-Post Gazette, The Journal of Poetry Therapy, One Trick Pony, The Potomac Review*, and was anthologized in *Pass/Fail*, a collection of thirty-eight teachers' stories. A featured author on poetrymagazine.com, Bates's work is also available at www.pitt.edu/~bbates.

LISA BEATMAN

Eulogy for Auntie Mame

Lisa Beatman was the first-place winner of the Lucidity Retreat poetry prize, and was awarded a Massachusetts Cultural Council Grant. She has attended artist residencies at the Tyrone Guthrie Arts Centre in Ireland, and the Writers Colony at Dairy Hollow in Arkansas. Her work has been published in *Lonely Planet*, the *Hawaii Pacific Review, Lilith Magazine, Abiko Quarterly, South Boston Literary Gazette, Rhino, Manzanita*, and *Sport Literate* magazine. Beatman's book, *Ladies' Night at the Blue Hill Spa*, was published by Bear House Publishing.

SANDE BORITZ BERGER

Laundry

Sande Boritz Berger, formerly the creative director and president of Videowave Productions, Inc., has published widely. Her writing appears in *Ophelia's Mom* by Nina Shandler, Ph.D., *Every Woman Has a Story* by Daryl Underhill, *The Chocolate for Women* series by Kay Allenbaugh, and most recently, *Cup of Courage* by Adams Media. She's completed a first novel about suburbia in the 1970s.

MARLO BROOKS
A New York Smile

Marlo Brooks was born and raised in San Diego, California. She writes a monthly e-column for www.soloops.com. She is completing her second book, *Wives of War: From the Hearts of Those Left Behind.* She and her husband, Shawn, live in Winchester, California, with their three children.

JIM CIHLAR
Hanging On

Jim Cihlar's poems have appeared in *Prairie Schooner, Minnesota Monthly,* and *James White Review.* In 2000, he won a Minnesota State Arts Board grant in poetry.

ROGER CROTTY
Growing Up in Irondale

Roger Crotty grew up on the South Side of Chicago with the help of his parents, his brother, and a lot of relatives. He has been writing for a long time, almost as long as he has been indulging his two other passions: reading and rooting for the Sox. Currently he lives in an old city neighborhood in Cincinnati, where his writing is encouraged by two excellent writers, his wife and his daughter.

WILLIAM C. DAVIS
Blueberry Memories

William C. Davis is a retired assistant professor of communication at Marist College, Poughkeepsie, New York, who previously spent twenty-four years with the IBM Corporation. Davis and his wife, Cora Mallory-Davis, are community volunteers and have received the Family of the Year award in Dutchess County, New York.

ANGELA DODSON
Patchwork of Love
A journalist for more than twenty-five years, primarily as a newspaper editor and more recently as a freelance editor, writer, and consultant, Angela Dodson is executive editor of *Black Issues Book Review*. She is also a community college instructor and host of a radio program about black Roman Catholics.

DENNIS DONOGHUE
Aunt Moe Gets Reborn
Dennis Donoghue's work has appeared in various journals, magazines, and anthologies. He teaches sixth graders in Salisbury, Massachusetts.

M. CECILE FORTE
The Power of the Triangle
M. Cecile Forte, Ph.D., is a corporate consultant and author of six books, including *Wise Women Don't Have Hot Flashes, They Have Power Surges!, A Woman's Wisdom*, and *Stolen Love* under her pseudonym, D. Reid Wallace.

KATHY LYNN HARRIS
A Cool Drink of Well Water
Kathy Lynn Harris, who has published essays, short stories, nonfiction magazine articles, and poetry, has completed her first novel and is working on her second. Harris grew up in South Texas, surrounded by family who thought nothing of hard work and hard times.

JANICE J. HEISS
The Gutter Gals
Janice J. Heiss's work has appeared in various publications, including *Urban Spaghetti, Limestone, Poetry Motel, Black Dirt, Women's Words, Passages North*, and the *Lullwater Review*. She lives and works in San Francisco.

JEFFREY HIGA

A Troublemaker Tells Secrets

Jeffrey Higa was born and raised in Hawaii and left his aunties at eighteen to attend school on the mainland. He graduated with a master of arts in creative writing from the University of Missouri–St. Louis, and has been published in *Zyzzyva, Sonora Review, Bamboo Ridge, Inside Asian-America,* and *Honolulu Magazine.* He misses his aunties and hopes they will visit him in Knoxville, Tennessee, where he is currently living with his wife and daughter. His e-mail address is: aunties@jeffhiga.com.

MARK HOLT-SHANNON

Blood Sense

Mark Holt-Shannon writes short fiction, memoir, and personal experience essays on stay-at-home fathering. He has read his essays on New Hampshire Public Radio's "What's Your Story?" Originally from California, he now lives in New Hampshire with his wife and two daughters. Holt-Shannon says he loves chasing English, and writing "Blood Sense," has been his most exhilarating and personal chase yet.

ONG JEN HONG (SANDRA M. YEE)

Rice Girls

A motivational speaker, writer, and natural health coach, Sandra M. Yee (Ong Jen Hong) leads workshops in self-healing and self-empowerment in Atlanta, Georgia. She is currently working on a book on natural self-help health care and another on the meals and the mayhem on which her family thrived, clinging to their Chinese roots in America. Visit her website at www.onewithall.net/hangon.

ESTHER IVEREM

Women of Fortitude

Esther Iverem, a cultural critic, essayist, and poet, is at work on a new book about black artists and aesthetics. After working for *The Washington Post, New York Newsday,* and *The New York Times,* she founded www.SeeingBlack.com, dedicated to the dissemination of reviews and news from a black perspective. She is the author of a book of poems and photographs, *The Time: Portrait of a Journey Home*, a contributor to numerous anthologies, as well as a recipient of a National Arts Journalism Fellowship.

BEVERLY JAMES
Tia Sonia
Beverly James is director of public relations and information at the Emory University School of Law. A graduate of Howard University, James spent thirteen years as a daily newspaper reporter and magazine editor. The native of Tela, Honduras, currently lives in Avondale Estates, Georgia.

PAMELA JOHNSON
Of Aunties and Oak Cabinets
Pamela Johnson, a contributing writer for *Essence*, is the author of *Tenderheaded: A Comb-Bending Collection of Hair Stories*.

SHAWN KENNEDY
Black Swan
Shawn Kennedy is a veteran journalist, who during her twenty-year career at *The New York Times* wrote news and feature stories for the newspaper's Metro, Style, and Business sections. As a freelance writer, her work has also appeared in *Black Enterprise*, *Emerge*, and *Savoy* magazines.

YANICK RICE LAMB
A Toast to Aunt Rose
Yanick Rice Lamb, who teaches journalism at Howard University, is the former editor in chief of *BET Weekend* and *Heart & Soul* magazines. She is completing a biography on tennis star Althea Gibson and cowriting a book on bid whist.

DOROTHY LAZARD
A Gift Given Is a Gift Received

Dorothy Lazard is a freelance writer whose work has appeared in *Go Girl! The Black Woman's Book of Travel and Adventure*, *Storming Heaven's Gate*, an anthology of literary journals, *Essence* magazine, *Pathfinders Travel* magazine, and a number of literary journals. She holds an MFA in creative nonfiction from Goucher College in Baltimore. Currently she is at work on a novel and a collection of personal essays. She lives in Oakland, California.

DOROTHY BLACKCROW MACK
Dragon Lady

Dorothy Blackcrow Mack has taught at the Illinois Institute of Technology, University of Michigan, Oglala Lakota College, and Linn-Benton Community College. She is a contributing editor at *Calyx* and has had works published in *Alabama Literary Review*, *Folio*, *Fireweed*, *The Literary Review*, *Savannah Literary Journal*, *Shaman's Drum*, *Side Show*, *Spa*, *Sun*, and *Zyzzyva*. Her poem "Wind Cave II: Time of Emergence" was nominated in 1996 for the Pushcart Prize. She recently moved to Depoe Bay, Oregon, to write full-time, turning her experience of marrying a Lakota spiritual leader and raising a sacred herd of buffalo into a memoir, *Belonging to the Black Crows*. Her website is www.dorothymack.com.

TARA L. MASIH
In Search of Silver

Tara L. Masih has published fiction, poetry, and essays in literary magazines (*Confrontation*, *Hayden's Ferry Review*, *New Millennium Writings*), anthologies, and on audiocassette. She has received awards, including the Lou P. Bunce Creative Writing Award and a finalist grant from the Massachusetts Cultural Council. Her story "Turtle Hunting" was nominated for a Pushcart Prize. Formerly an assistant editor for the national literary magazine *Stories*, she now works as a freelance book editor and writer in Andover, Massachusetts. She was a regular contributor to *The Indian-American* and *Masala* magazines.

MARY MARINO McCARTHY

Aunt Nellie's Trousseau

A former teacher and advocate on women's health, Mary Marino McCarthy is a former association director who enjoys capturing family stories.

REBECCA McCLANAHAN

Aunt Bessie's Secret Life

Rebecca McClanahan has published eight books, most recently *The Riddle Song and Other Rememberings* (essays), *Naked as Eve* (poetry), and *Word Painting: A Guide to Writing More Descriptively.* Her work has appeared in *The Best American Essays* and *The Best American Poetry,* and she has received a Pushcart Prize, the Wood Prize for Poetry, and the Carter Prize for the essay from Shenandoah. She lives in New York City and teaches in the MFA Program at Queens University in Charlotte and the Kenyon Review Writers Program. Check out her website at: www.mcclanmuse.com.

LALITA NORONHA

The Visit

Lalita Noronha is a research scientist, teacher, writer, and poet, originally from India. Her work has been widely published and has appeared in *Baltimore Sun, The Christian Science Monitor, The Baltimore Review, Potomac Review, Passager, Crab Orchard Review,* and *The Asian Pacific American Journal.* In addition, her work has appeared in anthologies, including *A Thousand Worlds, An Anthology of Indian Women Writers* (Aurat Press, 1998), *Great Writers, Great Stories, Writers from Maryland, Virginia and Washington, D.C.* (IM Press, 1999), *Get Well Wishes* (HarperSanFrancisco, 2000), and *2001 Science Fiction Poetry Anthology* (Anamnesis Press.) She has also twice won the Maryland Artscape Short Story Award in 1997 and in 2001, and won the Dorothy Daniels Award of the National League of American Pen Women, and Maryland Individual Artist Award in Fiction.

MICHELLE PINKARD

The Warden

Michelle Pinkard is best known for her award-winning work as a military affairs reporter and columnist at *The Times* of Shreveport, Louisiana. The Omaha, Nebraska, native recently left the newsroom to pursue a master's degree in creative writing at Morgan State University. Her first poetry collection, *The Eye of the Tornado: Fifty Poems for Rhyme and Reason*, has been published by La Caille Nous. Her work also has been published in *Elements Magazine, Poetry Motel, Ya' Sou! A Celebration Life, Love's Chance Magazine*, and *Struggle Magazine*. Pinkard is currently working on her second volume of poetry and a memoir. Her website is www.michellejpinkard.com.

IMANI POWELL

Zenda

Imani Powell is a writer and visual artist of African American and Caribbean descent. Her writing has appeared in *Essence* magazine, *The Source*, and Russell Simmon's *One World Magazine*. She lives, works, loves, and creates in New York City, her hometown.

M. J. ROSE

The Mystery Writer

M. J. Rose (www.mjrose.com) is the author of six books. Her novels include *Lip Service, In Fidelity, Flesh Tones*, and *Sheet Music*. She was raised in New York City, worked in advertising, and has written for Wired.com, *O: The Oprah Magazine, Poets & Writers* magazine, and *The Readerville Journal*.

YASMIN SHIRAZ

After Hatred Comes Understanding

Yasmin Shiraz is the author of *The Blueprint for My Girls: How to Build a Life Full of Determination, Courage and Self-Love* (Fireside/Simon&Schuster). She is the former publisher of *Mad Rhythms* magazine, the creator of the "Blueprint for My Girls" empowerment series, and the How to Get into the Entertainment Business tour that assists young people in pursuing their dreams. She has contributed articles to *Black Enterprise, Upscale, Impact,* and *EUR Extra!* She resides in the suburbs of Washington, D.C.

ENID SHOMER
Tropical Aunts
Enid Shomer's stories and poems have appeared in *The New Yorker, The Atlantic, Paris Review, Poetry,* as well as more than forty anthologies and texts. She is the author of *Stars at Noon: Poems from the Life of Jacqueline Cochran.* Her first book of stories, *Imaginary Men,* won the Iowa Prize and the LSU/Southern Review Award, both given annually for the best first collection of fiction by an American author. She has been visiting writer at the University of Arkansas, Florida State University, and Ohio State University.

SARAH BRACEY WHITE
My Other Mother
Sarah Bracey White, a writer, arts consultant, and motivational speaker is currently executive director of cultural affairs for the town of Green-burgh, New York. Her literary work includes a collection of poetry, *Feelings Brought to Surface,* many short stories, and several novels. Her latest, *Carolina Love Songs,* is set in South Carolina, where she was born and spent her early years. Her memoir piece, "Freedom Summer," was included in the anthology *Children of the Dream* (Simon & Schuster, 1999). Her essays have been published in *The New York Times, The Baltimore Afro American Newspaper,* and *The Journal News.*

About the Editor

INGRID STURGIS is editor of ESSENCE.com. With her first crit-
ically acclaimed book, *The Nubian Wedding Book: Words and Rituals
to Celebrate and Plan an African-American Wedding*, she has become a
pioneer in creating wedding celebrations that incorporate rituals
from the Black diaspora.

Ingrid has worked as an editor for *The Philadelphia Inquirer*,
Bridgewater Courier News, *Poughkeepsie Journal*, and *Middletown Times
Herald-Record*, as well as *BET Weekend* and *Savoy* magazines. She
has been interviewed by *Bride* magazine, and her work also has
appeared in *Emerge* and *Essence* magazines. In her latest journey
across the cultural spectrum, Ingrid examines family relationships
in *Aunties: Thirty-Five Writers Celebrate Their Other Mother*. A New York
native, Ingrid lives with her husband in New Jersey.